8 Steps to Overcoming
Mom Fatigue Syndrome

MOM

F🗨G

HANNAH KEELEY

America's #1 Mom Coach

Mom Fog:
8 Steps to Overcoming Mom Fatigue Syndrome

ISBN-13:978-1727284324
ISBN-10:1727284321

Copyright © 2019 by Team Keeley, LLC

Published by Team Keeley, LLC
10221 Krause Road, Suite #668
Chesterfield, VA 23832

This book is dedicated to the zebra tribe.
The ones with the big girl pants and steel-toed boots.
The ones who are changing the world.

MASTER MOM MANIFESTO

I am a Master Mom.

I'm one mom of many who are quietly changing the world.

We're not marching in protests or setting up media campaigns.
We don't have time for that.

While other moms are making excuses, we're getting results.
While other moms are dreaming, we're awake doing.
While they're griping, we're grinding.
While they complain, we conquer.

We don't believe in being just a mom (whatever that means).
We believe moms are the critical element that determines the
 destiny of generations.

People shrug us off, heaven backs us up,
and hell is terrified of us.

We realize the power within us is greater than anything that
can come at us, and because of this, we have the tendency to
do pretty radical things.
You can call us crazy, maniacs, rebels,
but you can't call us average.

Tell us we can't do it, then move out of the way and watch.

Because we can do all things through the power at work in us and through us.

We change the world as easily as we change diapers.

And we're not alone.

God has our back and the world is at our feet;

and we are stronger—together.

And we're growing—quickly.

We're Master Moms.

We don't allow excuses;
we push past them.
We don't hide from fear;
We rise above it.
We don't raise children;
We empower them.
We don't tolerate life.
We master it.

We are Master Moms.

MOM FOG
8 Steps to Overcoming Mom Fatigue Syndrome

I PAID $50,000 FOR THIS BOOK

I can't forget that day. I was visiting my parents and snuck into my daddy's office for a quick call with my editor. One of the biggest publishing companies in the world had given me $50,000 to write this book that you're holding in your hands right now. My manuscript had been delivered, and it was time for a routine call to make sure everything was running on schedule for publishing.

But I was not prepared for this call. Not. At. All.

"Hannah, we've been looking over the manuscript and we just have some reservations." I suddenly sat up a bit straighter in my chair and pulled the phone closer to my face.

"What sort of reservations?" I asked. "It's exactly what we talked about."

"Well," she stammered, "We think it's too empowering for moms." Those words felt like a punch to my gut.

"Too empowering?" I asked. "What is that supposed to mean?"

My editor (who by the way is NOT a mom) began explaining, "We just think a mom really needs help to do more practical stuff."

"Oh, I see," I replied, "like laundry, and cleaning, and raising kids, and managing time."

"Yes! Exactly!" she said. "We could help you with editing and even hire a ghost writer for you if you think you need it." I just shook my head and rolled my eyes. I'm glad it was a phone call and not a face-to-face.

"I included all the practical stuff," I said, "But let me explain something. A mom can't do any of that until she is first empowered to do it."

I could feel my face getting hot and my throat starting to get dry. I swallowed hard and then asked the question that sealed my fate—

"Answer me honestly," I asked. "Would I have to change any of the eight steps I laid out in the book?"

"Umm," she began, "most likely, yes."

For the next several days, I stewed over that one phrase—

IT'S TOO EMPOWERING FOR MOMS.

I firmly believe that moms are the most powerful people on this planet. They just don't realize it. The Mom Mastery Method™ was created to empower and equip moms to create abundant lives. These 8 critical steps have been proven to be effective in women's lives over and over. Moms who have been set free from overwhelm, anxiety, depression, anger, clutter, binge eating, crippling debt, abusive relationships, and so much more. If I compromised on the method, I would be compromising on those moms.

The decision was made.

I bought my publishing rights back from the company and

decided I would not sacrifice freedom for finances. And the awesome news? God has restored those finances and more.

What you are holding in your hands had to go through hell to get to you. So read every word!

But! A few important things before you get started.

One, the Mom Mastery Method™ works incrementally. In other words, you can't skip to the juicy parts. It's all juicy, and it all builds on itself. JLo started from the bottom and that's where we're going to start, too. To do it right, you have to start from the beginning.

Two, it's a God thing, not a religious thing. This method has nothing to do with denomination and it doesn't even care if you've never been to church a day in your life. God is bigger than a building. He loves you and He wants to help you create a life that rocks.

Three, you're not alone. This method has worked for thousands of moms, from those who want to tweak a few things to improve their lives, to those who are at the end of their rope. We're stronger, together. You are not alone in this process but surrounded and supported by other moms. We saved a spot just for you!

Now put on your big girl pants and strap on those steel-toed boots. Your life is about to change.

THE MOM MASTERY METHOD

✍ Chapter 1: What's Going On? ✍

I didn't think a simple pot of macaroni and cheese could create so much anxiety. I stared into the cloud of condensation rising from the pot on the stove, transfixed by the swirling pattern. Blowing through the fog, I watched it disperse and fade away, only to start billowing up within seconds.

'Sort of like my life,' I thought. Clouded over, nothing making sense, moving in slow motion, and all the feeble attempts followed by inevitable failure. No matter what I tried, the fog just kept coming back.

I shook myself back to reality, knowing I had seven hungry kids to feed. Grabbing three boxes of store-brand macaroni and cheese (thank the Lord they were three for $1), I tore them open, tossed the cheese powder packs aside, and dumped the noodles into the boiling water.

That was when it happened.

The lights turned off, the stove stopped heating, and the air conditioning quit running as the house grew strangely silent. Of course, any silence is strange in a big family, but this was an eerie, yet familiar silence.

The electric company turned off the power—again.

I braced myself for the inevitable.

"Mom? Mom? Mommmm?"

I heard several kids begin calling for me and running into the kitchen from various places in our tiny home. As they began filing in, I was trying to think of what I would tell them. How would I explain this? What story could I make up this time? I stared at the crunchy noodles floating in the water that was no longer boiling. What would we eat for lunch?

I quickly made up a story about how the electricity company must have screwed up. But I knew the truth. I had screwed up, again. It seemed no matter what I tried, or how hard I tried it, I kept going back to the same problems—no money in the bank, clutter everywhere, headaches, weight gain, and depression. Now here I was, flat broke and desperately in need of a working stove and air conditioning. Summers in Virginia are nothing to play around with. I just wanted to go back to bed and let someone else deal with my life. But that was just the problem—it was *my* life.

I let the noodles soften in the quickly cooling water, but we were left with a sad excuse for macaroni and cheese that day—chewy noodles with tiny lumps of orange powder. We sat in the dark, hot kitchen eating the strange orange substance. I tried to make jokes about it to reassure my kids, but I actually wanted to throw it out the window, along with all the dreams I ever had about being a happy, energetic, successful mom. I kept choking it down while sweat began to trickle down my back. My mind returned to that cloud of condensation floating above the pot. I felt like I was stuck there—in a fog. I was constantly exhausted, I couldn't think straight, I had no motivation, and no matter what I did I couldn't escape it.

I had no idea at the time, but I had a full-blown case of Mom Fatigue Syndrome.

The Chuck E. Cheese Mom

Ten years earlier, life looked totally different. Blair and I were engaged, and like most engaged couples, we had big hopes and dreams for our life together. But I had my own hopes and dreams, too. I wanted to be a mom. But not a regular mom. I wanted to be a cool mom ("Mean Girls" much?). And one night, I saw her— the cool mom.

We had gone on a date to Chuck E. Cheese. Why we went there as an engaged couple with no kids is still beyond me. Maybe it was for the skee-ball. But I distinctly remember that night. We were sitting in a booth watching a mouse with a lazy eye and a bad case of palsy singing rip-off pop music, and I saw HER. The cool mom! She walked in with three kids under 5. They were all blond and beautiful, with dazzling smiles and killer wardrobes. Yes, even the baby. She sat down at a table, with her trendy hair-cut and designer backpack (no goofy diaper bag for this woman) and did something I had rarely seen before. She actually had fun with her kids!

I couldn't get my eyes off her—seriously! She must have thought I was a such a creeper! But, I saw in this mysterious "Chuck E. Cheese Mom" everything I wanted to be in life.

Fast forward a decade later and I was eating half-cooked mac and cheese in a cluttered house with no electricity. What happened?

"Before Mom Mastery University I went to bed when I felt like it, got up when I absolutely had to, and then schlumped out the door. I was always tired and not interested in what was going on around me. I needed a nap in the afternoon because I felt like crap. I could feel myself sinking. After plugging in to the Mom Mastery Method I have hope. I have goals. I have energy and get so much done in a day! I laugh with my kids and have been planning meals and eating better. I also set a schedule to go to bed and get up in time to have 2 hours to calmly get ready. Plus, no more caffeine to get through the afternoon!"

—Laurie B.

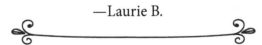

What's Going On?

The biggest problem with Mom Fatigue Syndrome is that you don't realize what's causing it, so there seems to be no way to fix it. You just keep putting bandages on the festering wounds. You try to get more sleep, you drown yourself in coffee and energy drinks, you indulge your sugar cravings, you pump up the vitamins and maybe even the prescription drugs. My go-to was Diet Mountain Dew. I was literally addicted to the stuff.

But the underlying fatigue just won't go away. It's not that you're sleepy. It's a tired that sleep can't fix. You're just stuck in a fog. And for moms, it's a very specific type of fog—the Mom Fog.

I am not a doctor. I'm a Mom Coach. I've dedicated years to researching this crazy phenomenon of Mom Fog that I saw in so many moms' lives, including my own.

One time I actually fell asleep while putting a fitted sheet on my child's bed after her 15th bed-wetting incident that week. One minute, I'm leaning over her bed pulling the corner of a fitted sheet over the mattress. The next minute, I'm drooling on it. True story.

Another time, while I was reading aloud to my children, I began verbally listing all of the ingredients on the shopping list that continually floats around in my subconscious. It went something like this: "Then Aragon snatched his sword out of the dwarf's firm grip and turned to face the oncoming horde of canned beans, diapers, spinach, toilet paper, apples, mozzarella cheese…"

I looked up to see my kids' faces staring at me in utter incredulity. I immediately took another swig of my coffee, slapped my face a few times, and continued with the story.

And every single breastfeeding mom on the planet can confess to falling asleep while nursing her baby. Half an hour after you begin nursing, your baby is fast asleep in your arms. And you're fast asleep with one naked boob hanging out, loud and proud for all the world to see.

And so goes the glamorous (and tired) life of motherhood.

But even more than the pervasive tendency to fall asleep every time you your butt makes contact with a surface is the all-encompassing feeling of being stuck in a fog. See if you can relate to any of these symptoms:

- You experience typical "momnesia," forgetting things so easily. You walk in a room and totally have no idea what you were going after.
- You don't process what your kids say to you. They're telling you all about their latest Lego creation, but you hear a series of multi-syllabic grunts, to which you respond, "Uh-huh."
- You are exhausted when you go to bed but can't sleep because your mind is stuck in "R & R"—reviewing all the stuff you didn't do and rehearsing all the stuff you've got to do.
- You have a "to do" list a mile long but no system to get it done so you're stuck just shuffling it around and feeling guilty.
- You work extremely hard but have absolutely nothing to show for it. The best you can come up with is, "I'm still breathing. The house is still standing. And all the kids are alive and accounted for."
- You tend to get depressed or suffer anxiety. And any mom

who has been there can tell you what a glorious hell-ride it is.

- And the biggest giveaway? You have zero motivation. It's not that you don't know what to do, you just have no desire to do it.

I could continue to list pages of symptoms, but if you're reading this book you already know what it feels like to be stuck in that miserable land of Mom Fatigue Syndrome. You're not yourself and sometimes you feel like you've forgotten who "yourself" is anyway. You want to be more and do more but can't summon up the energy, physically or emotionally. You're just stuck in a fog while the days melt into months, the months melt into years, and you wonder if your life is ever going to change. You wonder whether you're ever going to get your passion back, your moxie, your mojo. But, for now, you're just trying to crawl through the day.

I got you.

But I want *you* to get you. *And get the "true you" back!*

There's a very logical reason you feel stuck in a Mom Fog, and helpless to get out of it. And it all began back in 1965 when this guy named Martin Seligman started shocking dogs.

"Before applying the Mom Mastery Method, I had a terrible time getting up, dragged through my morning living on

caffeine, snacked to get me through the afternoon slump, didn't get lots accomplished so tasks got backed up. Now I have found a level of joyful energy I didn't even know existed! No caffeine required! I'm getting so much done each day with plenty of time for fun and work toward dreams becoming reality."

—Pam B.

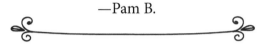

Help! I'm Helpless!

You may already be familiar with the work of Pavlov—the guy who could make dogs salivate just by ringing a bell, because he earlier paired the ringing of the bell to receiving a yummy treat. Which, by the way, is the same reason I start drooling when the chocolate chip cookies come out of the oven. The expectation of the stimulus creates the same reaction as the stimulus itself. Oven door opens + smell of cookies = drool (even though I haven't had a single bite).

Along comes Martin Seligman, an American psychologist who wanted to take Pavlov's research a bit further. But, instead of giving a positive stimulus like a yummy treat, he decided to go the more warped, twisted route and deliver an adverse stimulus—an electric shock.

Seligman would ring a bell and, at the same time, deliver a mild electric shock to a dog. The dogs who were conditioned to associate the bell with an electric shock would react to the bell the same way they did to the shock, pairing those two together. After this, he placed each dog in a box where it could escape the shock simply by jumping over a divider. He expected the dogs to jump over the divider when they heard the bell ring. But the results were alarming. He found that the dogs that were conditioned to receive the shock stayed on that side of the box and endured the punishment, often lying down and just taking it. However, when he put a dog that had never been shocked in the box and delivered a shock, it quickly jumped over the divider. I can see that dog right now, snatching off those gold hoops and shouting, *"Oh, no you di'nt!"*

The dogs that were conditioned to think there was no way to escape pain never tried to escape, even though escape was available—a phenomenon that Seligman, the anti-dog whisperer, labeled "Learned Helplessness." He defined this condition as, "not trying to get out of a negative situation because the past has taught you that you are helpless."

The escape was there for both dogs. One took it. The other did not.

Dogs that had learned they could not escape pain, stopped trying to escape from it. If they could talk, they would probably say, "Why even try? What good is it going to do? Nothing I do ever works out for me so I'll just sit here and take it."

It's also highly likely that this dog was wearing yoga pants and a frumpy t-shirt, with hair in a messy bun, scrolling through Instagram, and drinking a Diet Mountain Dew.

Learned Helplessness is not limited to dogs, as you have guessed by now. It's seen in people who have erroneously learned that trying equals failing. They feel like the little engine that could really can't so it won't. They have tried to escape their pain and improve their circumstances, but nothing seems to work, so they quit trying. Even though that breakthrough could be just around the corner.

People with Learned Helplessness exhibit some of these symptoms: passivity, low self-esteem, depression, hostility, anxiety, aggression, insomnia, confusion, lack of interest in activities, procrastination, decreased problem-solving ability, and... *chronic fatigue.*

Sound familiar?

"Before Mom Mastery University I thought I was going crazy, but now I know that I am crazy blessed! Thanks to Hannah and MMU I've grown as a mom. My whole family is strengthened and blessed by what I am learning."
— Jessica B.

Let's paint a little picture here. There's Mom—with stars in her eyes and dreams in her heart. But life doesn't quite play out the way she anticipated. She cleans the house and in 5 minutes, her kids have strewn toys all over the place. She eats healthy for a day but the kids want macaroni and cheese, so she eventually finds herself leaning over the kitchen sink gulping down leftover noodles (bonus points if the noodles are partially uncooked). She wants to be hot and sexy for her husband, but the smell of residual baby puke isn't necessarily the strongest aphrodisiac.

You see what's happening here? Learned Helplessness. No matter what she does, she can't seem to get ahead or change her circumstances. If her actions fail to yield sustaining results, then why continue taking action? Why not just curl up with Ben & Jerry and call it a day, or a night, or even a life? Energy? Focus? Drive? Action? … *Why?*

Hence, Mom Fatigue Syndrome.

And because this book magically ended up in your hands, I'm guessing you know what I'm talking about. And kudos to you for staying awake this long to read it! Now, I've got to break some news to you.

First, the bad news. You may be experiencing these same symptoms. You've tried and failed, and don't feel like trying anymore. You feel stuck. You want more but don't know what to do about it. And those big dreams of yours? You're torn between being terrified that they could actually happen and being terrified that they never will. You've resigned to live by default because living by design just isn't working out.

But it will never work out if you keep trying to change by picking yourself up by the bootstraps, making a list of your resolutions, gritting your teeth, and taking the typical "self-help" avenue. Those methods work great for some people. But you're not just some person. You're a mom. Your brain is even wired differently than other people (we'll talk more about that). These methods—the diets, planners, apps, budgets, programs, and all the other tactics you've been using—were never designed for you in the first place.

Now, the good news. What has been learned can be unlearned. It's not about *trying* to get it done right. It's about *learning how* to do it the right way (big fat diff!). You've got to change in a way that works with the life of a mom, which is distinctly different from the lives of other people. Yeah, Mom. You're an anomaly! But, that's cool. I can work with anomalies. Anyway, it's way more fun that way.

Chuck E. Cheese Mom, Part 2

I know what it's like to be in a Mom Fog. And I also know what it's like to be on the other side of it. After years of trial and effort, I finally discovered a method that works with the way a mom brain is wired—the Mom Mastery Method. It took years for me, but it's not going to take that long for you. Trust me. That's what this book is for. And it works.

Ten years after the mac and cheese episode, I took my kids to Chuck E. Cheese. It was valid this time—one of the kids had a birthday. We were all playing around together (I think it was near the Skee-ball), when a woman came over to me and tapped me on the arm.

I turned to see a young mother with three kids in tow.

"I'm sorry," she said. "But I can't quit watching you."

"What?" I responded, totally bewildered.

"You just seem to be having so much fun with your kids," she replied. "I really want what you've got."

I lost it. Seriously. Like tears, hugs, the works. She probably thought I had a serious hormonal imbalance by the way I reacted to her statement. But I was having a moment. It was as if God was giving me a glimpse of how far I'd come, all because I trusted His ways over my own. Those are the glimpses that drive me. You climb, and you climb, and you don't even realize how far you've come until someone taps you on the arm and you turn around to take in the breathtaking view.

You're going to have your moments. I promise. Now, take my hand. It's time to climb.

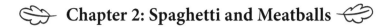 Chapter 2: Spaghetti and Meatballs

You've found yourself in The Matrix. Before you sits Morpheus, wearing sunglasses even though the room is dark. Sunglasses that by some strange, supernatural power stay on his face without any evident means of support. He stretches out his hands in front of you and opens them to reveal a pill in each one. A red pill in one hand, a blue pill in the other.

"Take the blue pill," says Morpheus, "and life stays perfectly normal. You know what to expect. It's predictable. You have a schedule that you can execute, a 'to do' list that you can get done, and a budget that works. You know what each day and each hour will bring, and you're prepared for it. You get adequate sleep. You do yard work on the weekends. Your socks match. Every now and then, you get a special night out on the town with fine dining. And you read books for pleasure, not survival."

"Take the red pill," says Morpheus as he leans in closer with a smirk, "and we throw some kids into the mix. You slowly forget what normal is. You cannot execute a schedule and your 'to do' list is hidden in a notebook that you can no longer locate. Your eyes, your boobs, and your bank account all leak uncontrollably. Your house becomes a toy minefield. You can sleep through a Category 4 tornado but can't sleep when your child is breathing heavy. You eat whatever is easily accessible and not overgrown with mold. All your laundry carries a faint scent of urine, and a night out means going to Target unaccompanied."

Sorry. You don't have a choice. You already took the red pill. So, let's stay in the Mother Matrix and find out how deep this rabbit hole goes, shall we?

Moms live dramatically different lives from other people. Our minds look like a Pinterest page of "random necessities"—no rhyme, no reason, but absolutely required. Moms can have conversations with other moms because minor emergencies or sporadic brain farts break up every other sentence. It's cool, though. We get each other. We have the same "squirrely" brain patterns.

There's a reason for this: Moms are MVPs. Non-moms are SCPs.

SCPs v MVPs

SCP stands for Singular Constant Professionals. These are people who can compartmentalize their lives. They can focus in a singular direction at a constant rate. These people have the capacity to go from A-Z without interruption. They have an internal control center, where they can create their structure and execute their plans.

SCPs typically have jobs outside the home. If they work within the home, they are primarily only responsible for themselves. They can create a plan and they have the capacity to execute it because they do not have unavoidable distractions. I once heard an interview with a well-known business leader about how he manages his time. He said he crams his calendar so full that he allots only seven minutes for a meeting. Spoken like a true, blue SCP! It's taken me more than seven minutes to clean a big, bad poopy diaper! And my child didn't even book an appointment with me. For a mom, operating on a schedule like that is somewhere on the same spectrum as coming home from a family vacation with clean laundry. Just. Ain't. Gonna. Happen.

MVP stands for Multi-Variable Professionals. These are moms, and they do not have the capacity to operate in a singular direction for a sustained period of time. The reason is because they have multiple variables coming at them from every direction. And they often can't delegate tasks or isolate themselves (You can't tell a baby with a poopy diaper to take care of it himself or come back and see you after your lunch break! Tried it. Doesn't work.)

We are all moms. We are all constantly pulled in a million different directions. Yet, somehow, some way, we are supposed to handle it like professionals. I got you, Girl. Let's do this thing together.

"This has been such an amazing program! I have learned so much, and my life is so much more peaceful as I have been implementing what I've been learning. I have vision for my life that I never dared dream about before, let alone write down and start pursuing!"

—Amanda S.

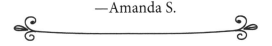

Most life-improvement programs—whether they are diets, budgets, marriage makeovers, decluttering programs, time-management systems, or any of the billion programs that moms purchase to improve their lives—are created by and for SCPs (not moms). They assume moms can stick to a schedule and maintain focus for more than 3.5 seconds.

SCPs and MVPs have two totally different thought patterns. SCPs can think linearly, in progression from start to finish. For example, they can plan a project, assemble the team, execute the steps, and wrap it up in style. Take dinner, for example. They can plan dinner, shop for ingredients, cook it all up, and even sit down and enjoy the meal. Novel idea, right? They don't have to do the "stop, start" dance that characterizes so much of a mom's life. MVPs like us are all over the place.

It's a bit like spaghetti and meatballs. SCPs are meatballs. They can operate in chunks—of time, energy, and thought. Moms like you and me, well, we're more like spaghetti—scattered and loose with the way we operate and think. But, this is out of necessity. Unlike many experts will tell you, this type of random, scattered thinking pattern is actually beneficial to moms. It's an evolved trait that helps us handle the inevitable distractions and pattern breaks that go along with motherhood.

And when you're a noodle trying to act like a meatball, you're doomed for failure.

Mom Brain is Real

I'm sure you've heard of "mom brain." It's this crazy thing that happens between our ears when we have kids—the scattered thinking, the forgetfulness, the occasional "who am I and where did all these kids come from?" brain farts. Mom Brain is the predecessor of Mom Fog, and it's just as real.

Physical changes occur in a woman's brain after she has children. When studying MRIs of moms, before and after they had given birth, researchers discovered a significant reduction in gray matter having to do with social cognition ("Pregnancy involves long-lasting changes in human brain structure," *Nature Neuroscience*, 2016). This is called "synaptic pruning." It's basically like the brain saying, "We have to figure out how to do all this new stuff, so let's make room and get rid of anything that's not vital." Responding to a baby's cry? Important. Speaking in complete sentences and remembering to put on clean underwear? Not so much.

Some experts say that Mom Brain isn't really a thing. Women who considered themselves to have foggy thinking actually performed much better cognitively in lab tests than they reported ("How do memory and attention change with pregnancy and childbirth?" *Journal of Clinical and Experimental Neuropsychology*, 2014). This leads one to surmise that maybe the changes were "all in their heads" and they were more functional than they thought. Typical meatball response! But, hey, here's a thought—

they were in a lab! They weren't in their homes where kids were grabbing at them, texts were coming through, and the laundry was scattered all over the place. Put a mom in her environment, and that gray matter starts shrinking.

Instead of fighting Mom Brain, start appreciating it! Our brain adapts to help us process new information when we become moms ("The maternal brain and its plasticity in humans," *Science Direct*, 2016). These changes help us to release our inner "noodle nature." We are able to respond more effectively and efficiently to random demands placed on our lives. Haven't you ever shocked yourself by the way you responded to some crazy event—catching that kid right before he runs in front of the car? Snatching that toy out of a baby's mouth when others didn't even know it was there? Having a "spidey sense" that your pre-teen was struggling?

The thing about Mom Brain is that we keep on trying to follow advice and direction from meatballs with all their gray matter still intact. That's when we try, and fail, and eventually start feeling crushed.

"I found Mom Mastery University while searching for a stress-reduction technique. After one of Hannah's programs I knew this was something I needed! Through the Mom Mastery Method, I learned how to live in faith and joy! I am so blessed to be part of this program and beyond excited to

help other moms discover the abundant lives that are just waiting for them!!"

—Sharon J.

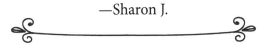

Help! I Can't Breathe!

As the youngest child in a pretty large family, I was always the one who got to squeeze into the least-desirable seat in the family car, whether it was the middle of the back seat, straddling the gear shift, or the storage space in the back of the VW bug. It was before the time of mandatory car seats and seatbelts, so don't call Child Protective Services on my parents.

Getting out of the car in the church parking lot was quite an event. The entire congregation would arrive early and gather around just to see that ratty old Volkswagen pull up, and to observe seven people extract themselves from it. It defied logic as well as automobile manufacturing guidelines. And I was always the last one out. It wasn't fun. I was squished, squeezed, and stuck.

Did you know you're in the same situation?

For too long now, you've been squeezed into a place you feel you can't escape from. The exhaustion you feel is just a side effect of the "squishing." Instead of trying to fix the exhaustion, we're going to cure the underlying problem. We're going to set you free and the energy will follow. You have enormous power and strength, it's just been contained, maybe even crushed.

In some countries, people train elephants through a process called "crushing." A large elephant can basically trample down anything in its path. Its strength is incredible! But in many cultures, in order to train these elephants, they take the babies from their mothers, place ropes around the babies' feet, and put them in boxes made of wooden slats. The elephants can see through the boxes but are not yet strong enough to break out of them. Every time they attempt to break out, they experience pain and quickly learn to stop trying.

They learn to become helpless.

Even when they are much bigger and stronger, they don't resist the trainers or struggle against the weak ropes that are holding them because of that familiar pain of their past. They hold back—massive strength held back by wimpy little ropes.

I know. Broke my heart, too.

But what breaks my heart even more is the millions of moms who have learned to keep their power in check. Unlimited potential breathed into them by God, yet held back by the wimpy, weak ropes of lies from the enemy. They have tried before and failed, so what's the point of trying anymore? I totally get it. Don't you?

How many times have you tried to improve your life? Think about the budgets, the decluttering programs, the organizing systems, the diets, the workout programs, the parenting systems, the marriage retreats. If it weren't for dissatisfied moms, I'm pretty sure Amazon Prime wouldn't even exist.

After a while, you just get sick and tired of trying any more. Reason? You experience pain every single time you attempt to fix it. And then on top of the pain, now you have a double heaping of failure because of the guilt that goes along with wasted time and money. Yeah, this is experience talking, Honey.

Welcome to the Club

I failed at seven (yes, seven) different home businesses. I tried at least a dozen exercise programs and more budgets and money makeovers than I can count (or add up on a calculator). I was on a new diet every lunar cycle. My husband was getting painfully accustomed to my monthly "next big thing." I even remember the day he strongly suggested I finish one of my other "life success" programs before I spent any money on another one. *Cringe.*

But what about all the testimonials; all the success stories? It worked for other people. Why wouldn't it work for me?

Has this ever happened to you? You bought a program, and because it was too difficult to execute with your current daily demands, you stopped trying. And then you felt guilty because you A) wasted money, and B) failed yet again.

One time I remember I heard this woman raving about an organizational system for plastic food containers. It was a Lazy Susan that held bottoms and tops in perfect order. I thought, 'Now THAT has got to work for me!' At the time, I had a huge laundry basket in my pantry that was overflowing with at least 87 pieces of plastic food containers—a mixture of tops and bottoms that broke every single law of averages by nothing fitting together, ever.

I hustled my buns over to Amazon and had that pretty little thing in my hands in two days. I set up my system, tossed out the laundry basket with all the old, mismatched plasticware, and began my journey toward leftover bliss.

Two weeks. That's all it took. After my kids had helped in the kitchen and made their meals, the Lazy Susan was in complete disarray. In the middle of complaining about my plastic catastrophe and trying for the umpteenth time to get it reorganized, it finally dawned on me. The woman who was raving about the system did not have any kids at home. It was her and her husband, and she didn't even cook the meals. No wonder it didn't work for me! It worked great for her. It was the bane of my existence.

Here's some breaking news for you—solutions for SCPs often become headaches for MVPs. What works for the SCP is likely to give the MVP a full-on anxiety attack. Life is not happy for a noodle who's trying to be a meatball!

It's not you that failed. The program failed you.

We don't work out the way others work out. Getting a gym

membership and starting an early morning high-intensity training class seems appealing, until you have a kid coughing up a lung, or you stay up all night working on a science fair project with your high schooler. Or you conjure up the sheer willpower to attend the class, but during the high-intensity jumps, your nursing pads fall out of your exercise bra and onto the floor right in front of Miguel, the cross-training coach who wears spandex on the daily. True story. Seriously, I can't make this stuff up. I never showed my face (or my nursing pads) in that class again!

Do you see how our lives cannot fit into a mold? Instead of trying to cram your life into a mold, and getting increasingly frustrated at your lack of results, why not just change the mold to fit your life? You're different. You're unique. You're an MVP and you need a program that will work for YOU!

But you can't move forward if you're stuck in the past. So, if you have tried and failed, and tried and failed, then let's just decide right now. That's over with. You're creating a brand-new life, establishing new methods, and getting new results. And there's no room for guilt on this journey. Let's drop kick that sucker out of your life right now.

God's mercy is new every morning (and fortunately for us, every moment). God loves fresh starts and new beginnings. He even tells us, "Behold, I am doing a new thing; now it springs forth, do you not perceive it…?" (Isaiah 43:19 ESV). He wants to do a new thing in your life. That's why you are holding this book in your hands. That's why we've joined forces. But you've got to perceive it. You've got to be willing to jump in and acknowledge that God wants more for you than sucking down Starbucks just to survive the day. He has designed you to live a full and satisfying life. That's why we're here hanging out together.

This is not just another book or program. This is about God orchestrating something amazing simply because He loves you so much and wants you to live the life He designed you for. And, no, guilt cannot come along for the ride.

"I had everything I thought I ever wanted, and still wasn't happy. My life was the story of Cinderella, backwards! That has all changed since Mom Mastery University. Pain has been replaced by empowerment. I want all moms to feel they can do this and do it well—and not put themselves last anymore."
—Kerry T.

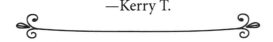

Romans 8:1 tells us "There is no condemnation for those who are in Christ Jesus." So let it go. If you have failed before, then join the club. Most pathways to success are paved with bricks of failure, so you're off to a great start.

Take my hand, step out of the past, and let's step on this crazy train together. You're going to discover why you are so amazingly unique and what will truly work to break out of the fog, create crystal clear clarity, and radically transform your life.

Be the Bread

Remember when bread makers were the bomb? Every household had a bread maker in the kitchen. I got one in 1998, and I'm pretty sure I gained like 14 pounds that year, just from bread alone. That was also the year loose-fitting cargo pants became popular. God is so good!

The great thing about a bread maker is that you can't get it wrong. As long as you know how to measure and flip a switch, you can bake delicious bread.

The thing about these eight steps is that they comprise a system—a system that works every time. And if you follow directions and jump in, you can create a delicious life—full of energy, joy, abundance, and productivity. And it's totally carb-free!

We're going to clear out that Mom Fog and create this life by following the eight steps of the Mom Mastery Method.

#1—**Massive Action**
#2—**Motivation**
#3—**Mission**
#4—**Mindset**
#5—**MAP**
#6—**Momentum**
#7—**Meditation**
#8—**Manifestation**

This is not just an idea, or a clever little list of words that begin with "M." This is actually a system that has worked with tens of thousands of moms to help them radically transform their lives. It works, but you've got to work it.

I promise you two things: You're going to get results, and you're going to have fun. So, let's get started with some Massive Action!

STEP ONE: MASSIVE ACTION

Chapter 3: Scratch It Up!

"Time to go!"

I'm sure you've said that to your children plenty of times. You may have been at the pool or at a friend's house, but more than likely, you got some kickback after you said it.

I'm sure God got some kickback from Abraham as well. Abraham had a huge promise over his life—he would be the father of many nations, and through him all nations would be blessed. Yeah, that was a pretty big deal. Because Abraham had such a huge future, he had to take a big step. The first thing God told him was to take Massive Action—"…Go for yourself [for your own advantage] away from your country, from your relatives and your father's house, to the land that I will show you" (Genesis 12:1 AMPC).

You will notice as you move out of where you are and into the abundant life God created you for, you're not going to be able to take everyone with you. God had to move Abraham out of where he was, away from the people he was used to hanging out with. For his entire life, Abraham had heard one way of thinking—a way that was without God and without hope. God was leading him to a new life, but first He had to get Abraham out of his small world.

It's also time for you to leave that small thinking behind and step into your new life. It's a massive step we are taking together. But you have a massive promise over your life.

Any Shoe Will Do

Now, I know your initial instinct before you do something big:

I've got to prepare for this!
I'll do it next month.
Let me get past this event first.
There's no room to take on one more thing.

In all honesty, there is NO "right" time to change your life. The right time is when you make that decision to jump in. And the more time you spend "prepping" the more time you take away from that abundant life that God called you to live.

One beautiful spring day, my daughter, Kenna, ran inside and yelled for me to come outside with her and check out these three owls she found sitting in a tree. Well, I was in the middle of cleaning the kitchen, going through the motions in a fog, and truly cared a whole lot less about the owls than I did about the gunk caked up around the edges of my sink. I was also barefoot.

"I don't have my shoes on, Honey!" I replied.

"So put them on!" she retorted. "You gotta see this!" Begrudgingly, I was still looking for an "out" to stay inside and keep cleaning.

I could Google pictures of owls. I couldn't Google a clean sink.

"I can't find my shoes," I said. "It's okay."

But my daughter persisted. She wasn't giving up. "Mom, come on! Find your shoes and let's go! They may not be there much longer."

I let out a deep sigh and went to the shoe bucket. With a large family, we need one central place where we can kick off our shoes when we come inside. Of course, shoes aren't the only things we find in there—dirty socks, loose change, small children. I half-heartedly shuffled through the shoes and couldn't find a match.

"Seriously, Sweetie. I can't find any shoes."

Then she adamantly snapped, "Any shoe will do! Let's go!"

I realized I wasn't getting out of this one. "Okay, fine!" I said. For my left foot, I grabbed one fancy sandal that was all studded with multi-colored rhinestones, and for my right foot a flat black Birkenstock. Now that was a look you would never find in Style magazine! I followed my daughter outside and after a short walk into the woods we got to the tree. She stopped, looked up, and pointed through the branches.

"Mom," she whispered. "Look right there."

I peered through the leaves and saw three adorable owls perched on the branches. One was tucked in near the trunk, and the other two were sitting farther out. The one on the outer edge was fluttering his wings and looking all around him. It was such a beautiful sight.

We stayed there in the woods for quite some time looking at the owls. We gave them names and personalities, and then began to make up stories about them. Even long after we returned to the house, we continued to tell wild stories of owl adventures. It certainly beat having a clean sink!

I'm sharing this with you because as moms, we tend to procrastinate when it comes to making changes—even those changes that would hugely benefit us. We make excuses for not jumping in. As strange as it sounds, we get comfortable with being uncomfortable. And, even though we want to snap out of the fog and create energy and abundance, we drag our feet because it's unknown territory. As oppressive as the fog feels, we stay there because we can't see beyond it.

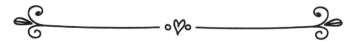

"Before the Mom Mastery Method, I could barely get out of bed I the morning. No matter how much I slept I would feel like I needed a nap in the afternoon. I went to my doctor because I thought something was wrong with me medically. He said that I was clear of any physical or mental illness. I was just tired. I didn't know what I was going to do. I had no motivation for anything. Then, when I felt like I had

nothing left, I found Hannah. She turned my life around. I have no problem getting up in the mornings, and no longer need a nap. My life changed thanks to Hannah and the Mom Mastery Method."

—Asia B.

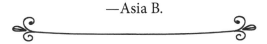

Your identity has been your identity for as long as you can remember. Maybe you labeled yourself as shy, distracted, or lazy. You may even have other labels that you're not even aware of—unlovable, unworthy, or broken. I'm telling you right now that you are already more than enough. As a child of the Most High God, you are an heir to the throne. His DNA is inside you. You are a daughter of the King. The goal of this first step is not to give you a new identity, but to realize who you already are.

As scary as it feels to move forward, I want you to be more scared of staying put. It's time for a change. It's time to do things God's way and reveal the brilliance hidden within you. Don't wait for things to be perfect because the perfect time is now. Your entire life has been building up to this. You've been prepping for years; maybe even decades. None of that time is wasted. The events you've been through, the mistakes you've made, the years you've lived in a fog, maybe even the trauma you may have suffered—God wastes none of it. Life didn't happen TO you, it happened FOR you; and it has all been leading you to this moment. You've already taken Massive Action by purchasing this book and making it all the way to the end of Chapter 3 (which is very rare for most people). You've already proven you're a cut above, now let's keep it going. It doesn't have to be perfect, it just has to be done.

So, let's get it done.

The Story Behind the Story

Renita heard about the Mom Mastery Method and wanted to use it to help her tackle her home. But here's the deal—Her home wasn't in bad shape. It wasn't perfect like a stuffy museum, but it sure wasn't a scene from "Hoarders." It was clean enough to be a house, messy enough to be a home. Stepping in to Renita's home would give you the impression that this woman had it together.

But don't let impressions fool you.

I got a chance to talk with Renita and she shared with me that she absolutely hated cleaning up her home.

"I feel like someone's maid or servant," she said.

"Did you have to clean up your room when you were younger?" I asked. This clearly fired her up.

"Oh my gosh!" she exclaimed. "It was horrible! Every single Saturday my mom would make all of us stay inside and clean up the house. We weren't allowed to do anything until it was all cleaned up. We couldn't even go outside."

Immediately I became aware of the real issue. She had developed a belief as a child that she was carrying over into her adult years. It's amazing how we get stuck in childhood stories and continue to tell them internally even though they no longer serve us as grown-up women. Such was the case with Renita.

"Do you see that you are doing the same thing to yourself?" I asked. "You've always seen cleaning as punishment; instead of putting it into a different context."

Renita looked at me wide-eyed and fell silent.

"Renita, you have big dreams for yourself, don't you?" She immediately reacted, her face broke out in a huge smile and she started nodding her head.

"Huge dreams!" she shouted. "Like so big it scares me."

"I know," I said. "And you are afraid of acting on those big dreams, so you use a safe excuse like housework to protect you. You see it as drudgery, and you're punishing yourself with it. Then you procrastinate with the housework, so you can't go outside and pursue your dreams. You have a valid excuse, even though it's not serving you. It's safe. You're comfortable with it."

I could see Renita's face soften as she took it all in.

I gently touched her shoulder. "Renita, you view housework as drudgery because you were forced to do it as a child. You're exerting your own control over it as a woman by procrastinating and refusing to do it. Meanwhile you are also using that excuse to validate not being allowed to go after your big, scary dreams. You're still behaving like a little girl even though you're a woman. Solve the little girl's problems and watch the woman's dreams come true."

I could see Renita look off into the distance, processing what I just told her. "You just nailed it," she said, slowly. "I have no idea how you did it. But that's so true."

"What if you changed the meaning you gave your housework?" I asked. Renita looked confused.

"What if instead of seeing yourself as a servant or a maid (which is how she felt as a child), you could see yourself as the queen of your castle, establishing your royal quarters? What if you designated a couple of hours in the morning to go after your dreams (go outside and play) before you started on your royal tidying? You would be getting things done but doing it your way. You're a grown woman, Renita. It's time to start establishing your own systems and writing your own stories."

Just like with Renita, many of us go through life playing out the same old storylines and saying the same old script, even though we have the power to create something brand new that would serve us better.

About a month later a post from Renita came through. She was standing in front of her tidied-up bedroom with a tiara perched on her head and the comment, "enjoying my royal chambers this morning!"

Renita had her breakthrough. Now it's time to get yours.

What's on Your Playlist?

My daughter cracked up laughing when she picked up my phone the other day.

"Mom," she said. "These music suggestions just popped up based on your recent listening choices—the *Trolls* soundtrack, Disney Princess songs, *Shrek*, *Newsies*, and *Weird Al's Greatest Hits*. Are you for real?"

It's true. My music tastes still looks as if I'm in the fourth grade. I'm not ashamed. Give me a good Disney singalong, and I'm perfectly content. And pitch-perfect, I might add. Just invite me to a karaoke party and play "Part of Your World" from *The Little Mermaid*. You'll see.

Listening to childish playlists on your phone is harmless. But when those internal playlists you developed as a child are still playing in your head long after you developed body odor and graduated out of your training bra, there's a problem.

"I am proof that the Mom Mastery Method is for mamas in

all seasons of life. I have grown in all areas of my life! I have gained confidence in all that God is calling me to do and have learned who I am and whom I belong to. I am also feeling crazy blessed!"

—Anne B.

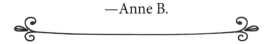

We live by patterns. We establish them (often at a young age); and they run on autopilot. Children's brains are much more malleable. It's called "neural plasticity," which means our thought patterns are easily created when our brains are more plastic and moldable. As we get older, these patterns become hard-wired into our brains, sort of like an operating system. But a big problem occurs when those established patterns are hurting us more than they're helping. Our thought patterns determine how we process situations and the meanings we apply to them. In other words, it truly is "all in your head." Your exhaustion and overwhelm have a lot more to do with the stories of your past than the realities of your present.

Our experiences create stories. The stories become our identity, which determine our thoughts. And we apply those thought patterns to everything that happens in our world. It's a bit like an Instagram filter. Our past creates a filter and everything that happens in our lives is filtered through it. Our thought patterns determine our mood, our energy level, our choices, everything.

Did you grow up with a story like Renita's? Where housework was punishment and it prevented you from doing what you truly wanted to do? Then that story becomes part of your identity. You become the "maid" or the "hired help." And you develop thought patterns that not only keep you surrounded by clutter and mess, but also keep you from fulfilling your dreams.

For too long, you've tried to alter your life by changing your choices. That's hard work. It's toil. It's strife. And it often results in gut-wrenching disappointment because it is completely counterintuitive. It goes against the operating system in your mind. Instead of changing your choices, why not alter the underlying thought patterns that determine your choices in the first place? It's as easy as creating a new playlist!

What's That Noise?

Have you ever heard something for so long you can just tune it out? When I was a little girl, our home had a cuckoo clock. I got so accustomed to hearing the familiar chime that I simply tuned it out. I could even sleep through it with no problem at all. However, if I had friends over, they would wake up every hour with that obnoxious "cu-ckoo!" resounding through our house. Needless to say, I didn't have a lot of friends over (I blamed it on the cuckoo clock).

We get used to what we continually hear and just process it like background noise. We simply filter it out. Many of these messages you encoded as a child, or through experiences in your past, simply run on a loop inside your head. They're internal dialogues which—although you originally processed them on a conscious level—have become part of your subconscious. You are no longer aware of them. But to a huge degree, they navigate everything in your life.

So, what are you sleeping through? What background playlist is running in your head? Do you have a cuckoo screeching at you? Because even though you think you've tuned it out and it's not affecting you, the reality is you are hearing it every single day on a much deeper level.

"I can sum up the Mom Mastery Method in one word— PEACE! Before MMU I was an overwhelmed, stressed-out, yelling mess. I now have peace in my mind, body, and soul. My kids are less stressed-out and overwhelmed, and my husband recently told me that he has to learn me all over, in a good way, because I am not even close to who I was 6 months ago."

—Heather M.

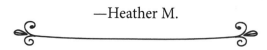

There are some playlists and dialogues that are continually running in your subconscious; and they are determining your choices. Let's take money, for example. What messages did you hear about money as you were growing up? Did you hear that money is hard to get, rich people are greedy, or there's not enough to go around? If so, then that can explain why you may have such difficulty with money now. If your subconscious believes that money equals pain, why would it allow you to make choices and decisions to pull more of that into your life?

Your subconscious is just carrying out orders. Whatever it has been taught, it finds a way to execute. Those money messages you heard as a child, and those money messages you keep repeating consciously, are just training your subconscious to create that reality. Money is hard? Then make money hard.

It's as if your subconscious is the crew of a ship and your conscious mind is the captain. You received messages and repeat messages on a conscious level and train your subconscious to carry them out. No matter how badly you want a change in your life, if you don't consciously act on it, your subconscious will just keep executing whatever it has been taught up to this point. Bad news? You've got to get to the root of the issue. Good news? It's totally doable!

Roots and Fruits

I'm the youngest of five siblings, and as a result, I was always the butt of their jokes. They were brilliant at persuasion and could make me do anything. My sisters once convinced me to eat three pieces of bread before a road trip so the bread would soak up all the pee in my body and we wouldn't have to stop for a bathroom break. Another time, they talked me into running after a horse (with a rider) that was trotting down the path and sniffing his backside with all my might to test if I had any horse allergies. Yeah, I was "that" kid—"Make Hannah do it. It'll be hilarious!"

One time, we were all outside and they convinced me to eat an "apple" from our neighbor's tree. Only, it wasn't an apple. It was a crabapple. Always eager to please, I grabbed the apple and took a huge bite, and immediately spit it out! It was so tart it practically turned my mouth turn inside out. They are pretty trees, but produce horrible, inedible fruit.

The thing is, you can't tell the difference between the two trees. Apple trees and crabapple trees look exactly alike—same trunk, branches, and leaves. You can only tell the difference in the fruit. Apples are delicious and nutritious. Crabapples are horrid!

Your subconscious is your identity. It's what you believe about yourself on the deepest level—who you are and what you can do. Because all of your behavior flows from your identity, your current situation (yes, even that exhaustion and overwhelm you experience as a mom) is a result of your choices. But your choices are a result of your identity.

So, if you've ever wondered why you try and try but nothing seems to change in your life, or why you start something great (a diet, relationship, life change) but then sabotage yourself, maybe we need to look a bit deeper. Sure, you can blame your choices. That's obvious. But the truth is you can only reach a level that your core identity believes is possible.

Proverbs 4:23 states, "Above all else, guard your heart, for everything you do flows from it." That's everything you do, not just some things. Every single thing that characterizes your life right now has flowed out of your heart. Now stick with me here because this little firecracker of a verse packs a whole lot of ammo.

The Hebrew word used here for heart is *leb*, which means "inner man." You have an inner man and an outer man, or for the benefit of this book—and inner mom and an outer mom. The outer mom is what is evident, the choices you make and the characteristics of the life you live: the fruit. But the inner mom is that deep identity underneath that determines the choices: the root. Everything you do flows from that root: the inner mom.

It's excruciatingly hard to change the fruit in your life—trying to start new habits or make new choices. It's much easier to just get straight to the root, the inner mom. Because if you can change that, you can change everything that flows from it. It's intuitive, simple, and natural. You're not going against the tide, you're flowing with a new one.

"I was the typical mom who was making changes from out outside-in. I had tried everything to lose weight—Weight Watchers, Nutrisystem, fad diets, nutrition counseling, vitamin B injections. You name it, I tried out. I plugged into the Mom Mastery Method and started making changes from the inside-out, and the weight just started falling off. So far I've lost 156 pounds! And it's still dropping!"

—Joanna H.

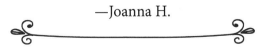

Let's take losing weight, for example—a struggle for many moms. Changing your eating habits and monitoring calories are difficult. It's counterintuitive because it's going against the wiring of your inner mom. If you identify yourself as an overweight person, you will continue to exhibit those behaviors of binging, giving in to cravings, and emotional eating patterns.

But what if you could get to the root? What if you could change your identity as "the fat mom" and start seeing yourself as "the healthy, light, energetic, strong, slim mom"? If you can change your identity, your behavior will follow that pattern. You will start seeing different fruit in your life. You will begin to crave healthier food, stop eating when you've satiated your hunger, and become more active in your life. It won't be as much work. It will just be a flow. Everything flows out of the heart. So, how do you change the heart and get that flow started?

Massive Action

As you know, the first step of the Mom Mastery Method is Massive Action, and that's where we begin. Sure! Every great journey starts with a single step. But we're not taking a single step. We're doing one of those leapfrog jumps!

My kids used to love watching The Wiggles Christmas DVD when they were little. But with all the wear and tear, it eventually got damaged. There were scratches on it, and as a result, we had to skip over one song because it was unplayable. Now, remember that old playlist you've been listening to? The one that's telling you that you're an overwhelmed, exhausted mom and doomed to remain that way? Yeah, that one. We're going to make it unplayable!

Just like that Wiggles DVD, your thought patterns need to be "scratched up" to create new ones. Remember, your entire life is an extension of your identity; what you believe about yourself. Many of those beliefs are limiting and have been holding you back from the life you want to live—the life of abundance, energy, clarity, joy, and immense productivity. Let's scratch up those old playlists so you can create a new identity, one that is in line with God's Word, one that reveals your true self—the mom who is at the top and not the bottom, the overcomer, the champion, the kick-butt warrior who is on track to create the life God designed her to live. You ready for this? Because first, it's going to require Massive Action.

When you are creating a life change, especially when you're breaking out of Mom Fatigue Syndrome, you cannot dabble your way out of it. You've got to dive right in. Dabbling is a waste of time and energy.

My son, Kyler, wanted to learn how to play guitar and he dabbled for over three years, showing up for weekly lessons and begrudgingly getting in his required practice time. At the end of three years, he could barely play a tune.

Then high school rolled around. A group of friends started a band and found out Kyler knew how to play guitar (I guess being able to play "Ode to Joy" qualifies as "knowing guitar"). Kyler, being hugely motivated by the opportunity to play in a real live garage band, started eating, drinking, and breathing guitar. Every morning I would hear that amp fire up. Within less than a month, he was playing guitar in a band, which led him to the position as lead guitar in our church's worship team. One time I even caught him playing a riff and leaping off the stage. It was a proud mom moment, even if he did rip his pants.

You can dabble for years and get nothing done. But when you decide to take Massive Action and do a cannonball into the pool of transformation, amazing things happen—*and happen quickly!*

Many people don't hit their resolutions or stick to their plans because they dabble with them. They tip toe in the shallow end and never go deep and follow through. You may be painfully aware of the effects of dabbling and "trying things out." As Yoda proverbially says, "Do. Or do not. There is no try."

You're a mom. I'm a mom. We don't have the time, energy, or money to dabble. You can spend years, decades even, dabbling and never get to the life you want to live. I want you to get results and that's why this book is in your hands right now. It's cannonball time!

Chapter 4: Altered State

There's broke. And then there's "I don't have anything to feed my kids and we just got a foreclosure notice in the mail" broke. We were the latter. We had a negative balance in our checking account, bill collectors calling, and maxed-out limits on all our credit cards. I had borrowed from everyone I knew, and I was officially out of resources.

We didn't know a lick about money management, and as a result, had run ourselves into financial ruin. My husband had been out of work for over six months. It was a desperate situation. We were on the verge of bankruptcy, my head pounded with stress, and my whole body felt like it had been hit by a truck. I'm pretty sure, if I had looked in a mirror, I would have seen LOSER stamped across my forehead.

For years, I had been thinking that if I just scrimped and saved and worked hard enough then we would have money. Then we would be wealthy, and we could finally feel free. I had no idea at the time that I was playing out a formula in my life that was destined for failure. It was the complete opposite of the formula for success that I'm going to share with you. I was living out a curse, even though I had access to a blessing.

Whatcha Workin' With?

There are two systems in operation—a worldly system and a heavenly system. I was operating by the worldly system because that's all I knew. I had impressed it upon my identity. And whatever you impress upon your identity, you express in your life. I was doing things backward and didn't even realize it. The worldly system can be summed up like this: If you DO then you will HAVE; so you can BE and finally FEEL.

It looks like this:

$$(DO \rightarrow HAVE) \rightarrow (BE \rightarrow FEEL)$$

You already know that you can't do anything that your identity doesn't agree to. I was trying to get out of debt and manage money better, but on the deepest level, I believed I was poor, broke, unable to manage money, and not one of the "lucky ones" whose lives were handed to them on a silver platter. Not only did I see myself as impoverished, I was jealous of anyone who had wealth. As hard as I worked, my identity was pushing money out of my life faster than my efforts could bring it in. I had the identity of a broke person. Therefore, no matter how hard I tried, I couldn't break out of poverty and lack. It was a mindset; a mindset that created my circumstances.

The world subscribes to this model. And it is broken. It's toil. It never works. It never has.

Proverbs 10:22 tells us that "The blessing of the Lord—it makes [truly] rich, and He adds no sorrow with it [neither does toiling increase it]" (AMPC). When God does something, He does it all the way. When He makes us rich, we're rich in every area of our lives—finances, energy, emotions, relationships, health. He covers it all!

"My 5-year-old son told me the other day that I was his 'new mom.' I told him I've always been his mom and he said, 'Yeah, but now you're nice and you're my new mom!' I cried tears of joy when I realized he has seen the changes, too."
—Akeisha D.

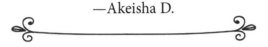

There was a curse over mankind, a curse that made life difficult and hard. But, Jesus redeemed us from that curse. "Christ purchased our freedom [redeeming us] from the curse (doom) of the Law [and its condemnation] by [Himself] becoming a curse for us..." (Galatians 3:13 AMPC). How amazing! Christ took all the pain and punishment of the curse so we could live with freedom. He picked us up and planted us right back in Eden. Because He paid the penalty, we can enjoy life as God designed it. Our identity in Him produces the rich life, not toil and effort. Everything flows out of that inner mom.

We need to adopt a new system, a new way of doing things, and it all starts with that massive step of changing our identities. God's system can be summed up like this: If you can BE that person God created you to be, you can FEEL what that person feels and DO what that person does; and as a result, you will HAVE what that person has.

It looks like this:

$$BE \rightarrow (FEEL \leftarrow \rightarrow DO) \rightarrow HAVE$$

I remember one Sunday my pastor, Dennis Lacheney, was preaching on money and said, "There are no shortcuts. It would be great if we could just take people who are great with money, draw their blood, put it in our veins, and suddenly we become excellent money managers. But that's not how it works."

He was joking, but there is actually some truth to that idea. When it comes to achieving success in life, whether it's breaking out of emotional bondage, becoming financially prosperous, or overcoming Mom Fatigue Syndrome, that massive first step is to switch up your identity. It's like getting a blood transfusion. You take the thought patterns and beliefs that have coursed through your mind for as long as you can remember, and inject your true identity in Christ. You get a transfusion of the blood of Jesus.

By taking Massive Action, I began to change how I saw myself. When those feelings of poverty and lack started to come upon me, I would remind myself who I am in God's eyes.

I am the head and not the tail.
I am the top and not the bottom.
I have access to kingdom wealth.
God supplies all my needs according to His riches.

His blessing makes me rich.
I am furnished in all abundance for every good work.

And it was working.

Inside-Out

Pretty soon, that Jesus blood began to work its way into my heart. I clearly remember the day when I had to go to the mall to run an errand. I entered through a department store and found myself right smack dab in the shoe department. Just months earlier, I would have stopped to ogle them and open a credit account so I could buy a pair. I rationalized it by saying, "Poor me! I don't ever get anything nice. I deserve these; it will ease the pain for a while and make me feel rich even though I don't have a penny in the bank."

But this time, I caught myself thinking something foreign. My first thought was, "So many shoes! I'm so grateful I'm already so abundantly blessed and don't need any," and I just kept on walking. Suddenly, I stopped dead in my tracks right between Michael Kors and Marc Jacobs. This foreign thought came out of MY head! The same head that had run us into over $200,000 of debt! I could hardly believe it. It felt so liberating to be free of lack. I was thinking like a rich person because that's who I was becoming! Instead of frittering away my money, I was learning to manage it, save it, and grow it.

"When I first came to Christ, I was rejected by my Hindu family and almost every person I cared about. I faced a tremendous amount of sickness and depression. My life fell apart. I tried to claw my way back but could never find traction. With the Mom Mastery Method, I finally have a strategy for moving forward in my life. Thank you, Hannah!"

—Pam P.

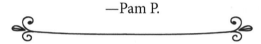

It's not that God doesn't want us to have nice things. He gives us all things to enjoy (1 Timothy 6:17). But He provides them, and He is the one to create that wealth in us and through us. It's not us desperately grabbing and groping for scraps from the table. He wants us to sit with Him and enjoy a feast!

My new way of thinking shocked me so much! I was becoming a brand-new person. God was making all things new, and I was perceiving it (Isaiah 43:19). I was doing things God's way—I was changing myself, and my circumstances were following suit. During those next few years, our finances changed dramatically. But it happened from the inside-out.

The world works from the outside-in, and it's like trying to roll a boulder up a hill. It's much easier to do things God's way and work from the inside-out. Roll that boulder downhill, Baby. And while you're at it, why not hop on and go for a ride?

What Is Your "Mom Identity?"

Changing your identity is always the foundation. And as you learn to "BE" that new person, you start "FEELING AND DOING" accordingly. However, here's the catch. The feeling and doing are interchangeable. To break out of Mom Fatigue Syndrome, you must have that identity of a mom who is energetic, excited, joyful, and living an abundant life. You can dig into God's Word and find out all about your new mom identity:

According to His Word, you are a strong, energetic, joyful woman:

"I have strength for all things in Christ Who empowers me [I am ready for anything and equal to anything through Him Who infuses inner strength into me; I am self-sufficient in Christ's sufficiency]"(Philippians 4:13 AMPC).

"But those who wait for the Lord [who expect, look for, and hope in Him] shall change *and* renew their strength *and* power; they shall lift their wings *and* mount up [close to God] as eagles [mount up to the sun]; they shall run and not be weary, they shall walk and not faint *or* become tired" (Isaiah 40:31 AMPC).

"...Be strong in the Lord [be empowered through your union with Him]; draw your strength from Him [that strength which His boundless might provides]" (Ephesians 6:10 AMPC).

"For by You I can run through a troop, and by my God I can leap over a wall" (Psalm 18:29 AMPC).

"May the God of your hope so fill you with all joy and peace in believing [through the experience of your faith] that by the power of the Holy Spirit you may abound *and* be overflowing (bubbling over) with hope" (Romans 15:13 AMPC).

"...Be not grieved *and* depressed, for the joy of the Lord is your strength *and* stronghold" (Nehemiah 8:10 AMPC).

"...Everlasting joy shall be upon their heads; they shall obtain joy and gladness, and sorrow and sighing shall flee away" (Isaiah 35:10 AMPC).

Change Your State, Change Your Mind

There is so much power in God's word to "re-educate" your inner mom on who she really is. However, as you begin to discover your true identity, you may find that things don't immediately fall into place. Just because with God you can leap over a wall (Psalm 18:29), doesn't necessarily mean you're going to feel like getting out of bed in the morning.

Knowledge is great. But knowledge without action is pointless. That is exactly why your awareness of who you are needs to be accompanied by action. Remember, BE is followed by DO and FEEL. Sometimes you can FEEL your way into DOING, but more than likely you need to DO your way into FEELING. Motion is always followed by emotion. Sometimes you wake up in the morning and feel like cleaning your house (I hear it happens on occasion). But usually you must start the motion and let the emotion follow. It's time to take Massive Action and change your state.

"I joined Mom Mastery University just to get a little help with my home but what ended up happening was my marriage moved to another level, I became stable in my emotions, I got amazing parenting advice, and a support network like no other and I've created some amazing friendships out of it. I'm also incredibly more productive in my home and in my life."

—Suzie G.

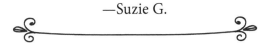

As moms, we often allow our circumstances to determine how we feel. But there is internal gravity just like there is external gravity. If we do not take measures to lift our emotions up, internal gravity will start to take effect and our emotions will sink to the lowest acceptable level. We've got to keep those emotions going strong to fuel our actions and get the results we're after. We need an emotional version of a push-up bra, Botox, and Spanx, all rolled into one!

Learning to alter your internal state is a Massive Action step. When you think about it, all your goals and dreams can be summed up in emotions. It's not really that you want to be debt-free; you want the way it will feel to be debt-free. It's not really that you want to lose those 30 pounds; you want to capture the way it will feel to be 30 pounds lighter. The real reason you want to have a better marriage, a clean house, or an organized closet, is the way they will make you feel. Our goals are representations of an emotional state. And when you learn to capture that emotional state, you send that goal rushing toward you in hyperspeed.

Trying to meet your goals with fatigue, hopelessness, and exhaustion is a painful process and rarely successful. It's opting in to the worldly system. But you have been redeemed from that. You have access to a supernatural system. Learn who you really are (and we will continue to work on that throughout the book), then apply Massive Action to get the emotion in place, and the motion will follow.

"That's awesome, Hannah, but I can't just get happy and energetic."

Remember, for too long you may have allowed your circumstances to determine your state. Let me show you how to change your state to determine your circumstances. Sitting around recreating your identity won't do you much good if you don't take action to solidify it and start getting results. We're moms. We don't have time to sit around and do any navel-gazing. Anyway, the stretch marks are much too distracting.

1. Change Your Body

Think about that typical mom who is suffering from Mom Fatigue Syndrome (MFS). How is she holding her body? Where is her gaze? How is her voice? How is she breathing? When it comes to MFS, everything gets depressed—activity level, mood, posture, voice, everything! When you start altering the physical symptoms, you start the motion of altering the emotional symptoms.

As you begin to change your body, you may be thinking, 'But Hannah, isn't this kinda faking it? Like I still feel overwhelmed and exhausted.'

Well, here's the truth. Your body has a difficult time discriminating between mental and physical energy. Your mind, body, and spirit are all one unit and will go toward the strongest pull. If you put your body into a state, your mind will follow. You can actually "trick" your body into excitement, strength, happiness, and positivity when you start replicating those physical expressions. Pretty soon, you're not faking it. Twenty minutes in, and you actually make it. You are being authentic. You feel like a more empowered woman because you are!

"But, I can't do anything about my feelings. I've tried."

Most moms try to alter their emotions on an emotional level. You can't battle emotions with emotions. That just doesn't work. It's on the same playing field and it often starts a spiral that doesn't end. You can't "think" your way out of a mind problem. Lethargy, overwhelm, exhaustion, depression, anxiety—all of these are mind problems. You need to get the advantage and raise the battle to a higher plane.

In sword fighting, if you can get a higher platform, you have an advantage over your opponent. The same is true for MFS. To overcome the mind battle, you need to step up to a higher platform and put the power of your body into the fight. You can consciously change your body even when you can't consciously change your emotions.

Consider the way an empowered mom holds her body, how she speaks and breathes, the expression on her face, her posture, and her gaze. One by one, start to alter these aspects of your body.

- Where is your gaze? Is it level or higher (now downcast)?
- How is your posture? Are your shoulders rolled back, chin up, neck long, back straight?
- How is your breathing? Is it deep and powerful (not shallow)? Try my "Magic 7 Breath": Take a deep breath in from your belly for 7 counts, hold for 7 counts, and then slowly exhale for 7 counts. Repeat several times. This helps to oxygenate your body.
- How are you holding your face? Are your facial muscles lifted and alert? Are you smiling? Are your eyes wide open?

Don't just sit there and pass this off. I triple-dog-dare you to stop, stand up, and follow through. Remember, knowledge without action is pointless.

Think I'm making all this up? Amy Cuddy, a social psychologist at Harvard Business School, discovered that just 2 minutes of "power posing" can alter the body chemistry, allowing the person to feel more empowered and willing to take risks. You've seen Wonder Woman do this power posing all the time—hands on hips, feet apart, chin up, shoulders back, and ready to take on the world! Go get 'em, Tiger!

It's Hype Time

Remember how you need to "scratch up" the old thought pattern? When you find yourself going down the negative road with your thoughts, 'I can't do this. I'm overwhelmed. I'll never get this right. I'm exhausted,' it's time to take drastic action! Put the Massive Action step of "pattern interrupt" to work for you.

Here's how it works—first, you realize there is a negative thought pattern happening. Here's a clue—Whenever you are feeling stress, frustration, or despair, or even bodily aches and pains, a disempowering thought pattern is behind it. Now, many therapists would say to take a moment to look inward and discover what that thought pattern is. But I know what mom life is like. We don't have time for that; we need to do what works now. Therapy could take years, or it could take minutes. But, the end result is the same. You want to weaken that disempowering thought pattern and create a new, more empowering one.

"I struggled with my weight since I was 19. One thing that I was really self-conscious about was my legs. I have larger thighs. I learned through the Mom Mastery Method to turn

off that negative playlist. Mine was playing, 'do not wear shorts.' For the first time in 15 years I am rocking my shorts! I feel great! I love everything about my body. And I'm crazy blessed!"

—Melissa M.

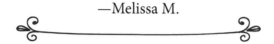

This is not only a way to interrupt a thought pattern. Sometimes all we need to do as moms is add a little "hype," something to empower and elevate us. It could be an energetic song, a silly dance, or anything to hype things up. When I'm getting ready to speak to a crowd, I often put on something like Twisted Sister, "We're Not Gonna Take It" and dance around the hotel room playing air guitar. I'm getting psyched up to stick it to the devil and I'm not going to take his lies anymore.

When you become aware that you are spiraling downward, take fast action and interrupt it with the craziest action you can think of. It's like pattern interrupt on steroids, and sometimes that's exactly what a mom needs. Do something totally out of the norm. Remember, it often takes something radical—more than just deep breathing or altering your body. Plus, the kids love doing it with you!

Here are some ideas:

- Do a Tarzan yell.
- Sing and dance to something loud and fast.
- Jump on the furniture.

- Put on drumline music and march around the house.
- Lie outside on a blanket for 5 minutes.
- Do a cartwheel or roll around on the floor.
- Make up a "mom cheer" and do it—loud!
- Scream "Yes! Yes! Yes!" while fist-pumping.

Let's go ahead and clarify something. Yes, you will feel foolish. Yes, you will look stupid. Yes, you will initially shy away from doing this. But, that's the whole point. It's crazy enough to interrupt the thought patterns that have kept you imprisoned for so long. You want that crazy blessed life? Then you gotta be willing to look a little crazy.

Second Corinthians 5:13 tells us, "If it seems we're crazy, it is to bring glory to God." Let that become your theme verse. You can either fit into the masses of moms who are overwhelmed and frustrated, or you can be radical and do what you need to do to live the life you want to live. So, c'mon. Get crazy.

 ## 2. Change Your Language

When my daughter, Klara, was about six years old, she came down with a horrible throat infection. She had a fever, and her entire mouth and throat were covered with blisters. It was excruciating, especially for such a small child. She asked for paper and pencil while she was lying under blankets on the sofa. After a while, I went over to see what she was creating. What I saw stunned me.

She drew a picture of herself with a drink in one hand and a heart balloon in the other. A big smile was on her face and written across the top of the paper were these words:

I FEAL BETTER THEN AVER!

I asked her about it and she told me that she wasn't going to listen to her body. Instead, she was going to tell her body how to feel. Mind = Blown! Even though her spelling needed work, her logic was spot-on!

There is so much power in the language you use. You just need to know how to use it. Turn on the filtration system in your head because your life goes where your words direct it. Many of us have filtration systems in our homes. Perhaps you have an air filter that keeps the dust and debris out of your home, or a water filter that keeps your drinking water clean and toxin-free. If we're that careful to make sure our water and air are healthy, then we can put the same effort behind the words coming out of our mouths.

Proverbs 18:21 tells us, "Death and life are in the power of the tongue, and they who indulge in it shall eat the fruit of it." The law of sowing and reaping is just that—a law. Whatever you sow, you reap. God invented karma before karma existed. It's called cause and effect, sowing and reaping. It's a spiritual law. Every word out of our mouths is a seed and it will result in a harvest. Many people aren't too happy with their harvest right now, but we are living the results of the words we have spoken. You make the choice—blessing or cursing, life or death, abundance or scarcity, peace or stress. Whatever you choose to plant, you will reap the harvest.

"My self-talk was terrible. I walked around constantly saying, 'I am fat, ugly, lazy, stupid, not good enough.' I told myself I was a failure—as a wife, mother, person. After plugging in to the Mom Mastery Method, I decided that every time I walked past a mirror, I would say something positive about myself. Suddenly, my life became amazing! I was smiling constantly. My husband noticed and started genuinely complimenting me. I have always tried to be positive, but changing my mindset changed my life."

—Marie T.

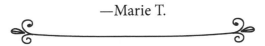

Words are powerful. Words created the universe. God spoke and—BAM!—creation! When God created the universe, He was also modeling how we create as well. Thoughts are energy, but that energy becomes tangible once we speak it. The Spirit of God was hovering over the darkness. It wasn't until God spoke, that manifestation happened. We're manifesting all the time; so be careful, little mouth, what you say.

Mark 11:23 tells us that "…Whoever says to this mountain, be lifted up and thrown into the sea! and does not doubt at all in his heart but believes that what he says will take place, it will be done for him." Often, we tend to talk to God about our mountains, rather than talk to our mountains about God. God gave us the power and authority to create an abundant life; and He says that we can have whatever we say, not whatever we want, but whatever we say.

Is That Your Confession?

Putting that filter over my mouth was one of the hardest things I've ever done. But I knew I needed to do it because manifestation comes out of confession. If the enemy can get you to confess something, then he has the legal right to stick it in your life. I wanted to change it, but disempowering statements would continually come out of my mouth. Things like:

I can't take it anymore.
Just my luck!
I'm sick and tired of _____.
I am so overwhelmed.
I'm exhausted.
I never get a break.

I was stuck in the same old thought patterns, and it was evident in how I spoke. It took me a while to realize that nothing was going to change about my life until I changed my language. Finally, I decided to do something about it. Every time I would hear a negative statement come out of my mouth, I would quickly follow it by saying aloud, "Is that my confession?" It made me stop, repent from that statement, and turn it into a praise. I also got my family on board. Every time someone said something negative, anyone who heard it was allowed to say, "Is that your confession?" Our language changed—drastically. It even got down to the nitty-gritty:

Me: This traffic is terrible!
Kid: Is that your confession?
Me: No! I repent of that. God is making a way where there is no way. Thank You, Jesus!

I did a whole lot of repenting, a whole lot of praising, and my life started doing a whole lot of transforming!

3: Change Your Focus

Have you ever thought about what you think about? It's called metacognition, and it's actually a thing, even though it sounds like it came right out of a Dr. Seuss book, "'Think about thinking about what you think about,' said the Barbaloots in their Barbaloot suits, sitting in the Truffula trees."

But if you can raise your awareness to stop and examine your thoughts, you then step into a position of being able to radically transform them.

Many moms blame their lives on fate—it's in my genes, I've just never been organized, I've got attention problems, I'm not good at relationships, I'm impatient by nature, I just take on too much." But the truth, as you have learned, is there are unconscious forces shaping our identities and guiding our choices. Carl Jung once said, "Until you make the unconscious conscious, it will direct your life and you will call it fate."

When you can stop and examine your thoughts, you are that much closer to making the unconscious conscious. You will be able to stop blaming your fate and start living out your destiny.

When those red flags pop up in your emotions—frustration, stress, anxiety, overwhelm, despair, aches and pains—it's time to whip out the big guns and do some metacognition. Can you hear those playlists in your head?

I'm not good enough.
I can't do anything right.
I never finish what I start.
I'm a horrible mom.
These kids drive me crazy.
No one ever helps me out.
I'm sick and tired.

When you think about what you are thinking about, it's as if you are the attorney listening to yourself in the witness chair. You can't change what you're saying, you've just pried enough to hear the testimony and get the truth. Now it's time to put on the robe, pick up the gavel, and step up to the judge's seat.

You have the power to determine whether you allow that evidence or not. You can bang that gavel down anytime you choose. When you detect, "These kids drive me crazy," you can hit the bench and say, "My children are a gift and a reward from God. They bring me happiness, blessing, and fortune" (Psalm 127:3). You have the power to overrule anything that surfaces in that witness stand.

"I was just existing through life, I never dreamed before finding Mom Mastery University because I thought dreaming just brought disappointment. Now I can honestly say I feel alive, I found my voice, my kids are thriving, my marriage is moving forward and I LIKE who I am!"
—Theresa V.

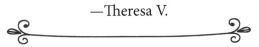

So let's start CROSS-examining your thoughts by holding them up to the cross of Jesus. Sometimes you can only detect lies if you hold them up to the truth, especially lies you have lived with for so long that—to you—they seem real. One way to cross-examine and discover empowering truths is to start asking empowering questions:

- Why am I doing this?
  Think about the processes you are working on to improve your life, e.g., going through the Mom Mastery Method, exercising, budgeting, eating healthy, and why you began in the first place. It may be for your children, your future, but most likely, it is for that amazing woman God created you to

be. Find your "why" and let it empower you to keep going.

- What is the outcome?
  Think about what your end result will be—a happy, energetic, productive mom. Spend time visualizing it and experiencing the outcome. What do you see? What do you hear? How do you feel? Capture the outcome.

- What am I thankful for?
  Often we get too caught up in the details of life and lose sight of the big picture. Gratitude is powerful. Turn the tide on negativity by giving thanks.

- How can I enjoy this?
  When we're going through a slump or breaking out of a pattern, we forget that we have the power to interject fun anytime we choose. It's like having a power outage and turning it into a game of "hide and seek" in the dark. You can curse the darkness or you can drive it away with light. Instead of thinking, 'How can I get through this? Think, 'How can I enjoy this?' Joy confuses the enemy. The devil will try to put junk on you to bring you down, but if you bring joy into the situation, the devil will be forced to go and take his junk with him!

- If I were already _____, how would I act right now?
  I call this the "Princess Mia Effect." In Princess Diaries 2, Princess Mia (played by Anne Hathaway) was addressing a crowd of poor orphan girls. She said, "To be a princess, you've got to believe that you're a princess. You've got to walk

the way you think a princess should walk. So think tall, smile and wave, and just have fun." There is power in assuming a role—you reach it more quickly and have fun in the process. So, you may think, 'If I were already an energetic, happy, peaceful mom, how would I act right now?' Then put on a performance that is Oscar-worthy!

Jenni, a mom who went through the Mom Mastery Method, used this technique to create a radical transformation. For her entire adult life, she was labeled as clinically OCD. She would not part with any gifts for fear that it would cause some horrible event to happen in the giver's life, falsely assuming her action—or inaction—would create uncontrollable chaos. Hence, her home was filled with clutter. She had kept a box of cookies her mother gave her (long expired) on her kitchen counter for over 20 years.

One day, Jenni sat staring at the cookies and asked herself, 'If I were already a mom with a clean house, how would I act right now?' Then, with her heart pounding out of her chest, she grabbed the cookies and tossed them in the trash. It isn't always comfortable and it sure ain't easy. But your future—and your freedom—are worth it. Do what you need to do to have the life you were born to live.

Lifestyles of Rockstar Moms

When I was a kid, I fantasized about being the Bionic Woman. I actually started a Bionic Woman fan club when I was ten, and would spend hours outside pretending like I could push cars over, throw boulders, and run lightning fast (If only it had been captured on video, I would have been a YouTube sensation!). We all played pretend as kids. Well, now we're going to play it again.

"Hannah, I'm too old for that."

I'm not saying that you and I must go outside, put cars in neutral, and push them down the driveway. I'm saying God created you in His image. You were made in the image of the Creator Himself. He even said, "…Nothing they have imagined they can do will be impossible for them" (Genesis 11:6 AMPC). Put your imagination to work and let's make the impossible, possible!

Imagine a reality show called, "Lifestyles of Rock Star Moms." This Hollywood production company heard about your awesomeness and wants to spend a day filming at your house. They want to show the public how you do what you do, how you rock your awesome mom life, how you get so much done, how you treat your kids, how you manage your home. If this were the case, what would you do? How would you manage your day? Your time? Your home? Your family? Your emotions? When you know more is at stake than just you, it changes your perspective. And the things you thought you couldn't do, you can now do with ease.

Truthfully, you are not doing this for just for you. You may have bought this book to help yourself; but the truth is, by going through this program, you are changing your home, family, and the lives of generations that will come after you. Perhaps this is the moment for which you have been created!

Go ahead and play pretend. This is another way to instill Massive Action to create real, lasting change.

Lights!

Camera!

Massive Action!

STEP TWO: MOTIVATION

 Chapter 5: Wha Choo Lookin' At?

I was 12 years old, sitting in the back of my dad's car, my arms folded across my chest and anger written all over my face. I left the house that morning on a bad note. I "smarted off" (that's southern for speaking arrogantly). My dad reprimanded me, and instead of cooling off on the car ride to school, I was letting it simmer.

The entire car ride was silent. I was pouting. And in my childlike mind, I was thinking that my dad was feeling remorse about how horrible he had treated his precious child that morning. Actually, he was probably thinking about a client meeting he had later that day.

He slowly pulled up to the front of the school to drop me off. I grabbed the handle, ready to make my quick escape.

"Nope," he said. "You've got to say it first."

"I don't feel like it," I said through gritted teeth.

"It doesn't matter whether you feel like it or not," he remarked. "You're going to say it before you get out of this car."

That just made me angrier. I shoved my arms tighter across my chest and scowled as hard as my childish face would allow.

Silence.

"Hannah, we'll sit here as long as you like," he said. "But you're not leaving until you say it." I could see the other schoolchildren beginning to stare into the car and a line of cars was forming behind us. I was going to have to swallow my pride and do it.

Through a clenched jaw, I muttered the words, "Anything I can vividly imagine, ardently desire, sincerely believe, and enthusiastically act upon, must inevitably come to pass."

I grabbed the handle and swung the car door open.

"Have a good day!" my dad hollered with sarcasm in his voice, just before I slammed the door and walked inside.

My dad once ran across that quote by Paul Meyer that changed his life. When he realized that he had ultimate control over his life, it greatly impacted him, and he wanted to pass along that wisdom to his children. He made us learn the quote and recite it every single day on the way to school. In fact, we couldn't get out of the car until we said it.

My dad understood the importance of vision. As a 12-year-old, I was more concerned with glittery lip gloss. But now I can look back and say, "Father knows best."

The Power of Vision

Can you vividly imagine where you are headed? Most people vividly imagine their futures, but completely unintentionally. They are imagining tough days, frustrating demands, tight money and tight waistbands. They are just projecting more of what they have already experienced. Therefore, they keep getting more of what they currently have. Make sense? It's an endless cycle; and you've probably felt that way as a mom. This is natural. But, remember, we are not conforming to the pattern of this world, we are being transformed by the renewing of our minds (Romans 12:2).

Although the natural response is the easiest, it's usually the one that gets us in the most trouble. My natural response as a child was to pout and bring more misery into my life. My dad forced me to do the unnatural. And even though I resented it at the time, I realize now what a blessing it was to instill that truth into me. But, as grown women, we don't have anyone riding our backs, helping us create a vision for our lives. So, we often take the easiest path. But that easy path is just a circle, never leading anywhere.

One of my favorite movies is *Mary Poppins*. During one scene, Mary, Bert, Jane, and Michael jumped into a sidewalk chalk picture and were magically transported to a country fair. They all grabbed a seat on a merry-go-round when Bert leaned back and remarked about it being, "Very nice indeed, if you don't wanna go nowhere."

Mary Poppins then replied, "Who says we're not going anywhere?" and she and her merry-go-round horse leaped off the platform and led the group of riders across the countryside.

As a mom, you may feel stuck going in circles, although it's not a nice merry-go-round. Sometimes it's like a Scream Machine! The scenery never changes, and the pressure never lightens up. Truth is, you may be surrounded by people who "don't wanna go nowhere." But I know you. You're ready to jump off and get going. Otherwise, you wouldn't even have this book in your hands. You know God made you for more; you're ready for it. Massive Action will help you leap off, but you need Motivation to go anywhere. And that is the second step of the Mom Mastery Method: Motivation

Stars and Sand

Motivation always begins with vision. There's a reason that the quote that shaped much of my childhood and my adult life begins with, "Anything I can vividly imagine..." Every great story, and every great life, begins with vision.

Proverbs 29:18 tells us, "Where there is no vision, the people perish..." It's true, too. Lives are perishing every single day because of one thing—lack of vision. This is especially true for moms because there are multiple variables that continually seek our attention (as MVPs), and it's hard, if not impossible to think beyond the urgent. But, if you don't take the time to fireproof your life, you're going to spend every single day putting out fires.

Developing yourself means making yourself fire-proof. You'll be able to think clearer, get more done, and have fun doing it. But, first you need vision. You need to see beyond where you are right now.

"The Mom Mastery Method has been a life changer for our whole family. When my wife signed up for it, I was not sure what to expect. My wife shared the process with us and had us work through the steps along with her. It helped us work through individual limiting beliefs but then took it a step further to teach us how to bring what we want into our lives. We've seen both substantial financial improvement as well as personal growth changes. I feel like our marriage is stronger as is our relationship with our kids. Even our 16-year-old is quoting Hannah!"

—Lucas J (Wrylon's husband)

It was only after Abraham took Massive Action and left his home town that God began working on the next step—creating a vision. God knew Abraham had to get something in his head to replace the old images. And in His awesome, classy way, He took care of business.

"In blessing I will bless you and in multiplying I will multiply your descendants like the stars of the heavens and like the sand on the seashore. And your Seed (Heir) will possess the gate of

His enemies" (Genesis 22:17 AMPC).

And to make sure that image stuck, God even led him outside to get a good look.

"And He brought him outside [his tent into the starlight] and said, Look now toward the heavens and count the stars—if you are able to number them. Then He said to him, So shall your descendants be" (Genesis 15:5 AMPC).

Abraham got a clear picture of his future—stars and sand. God showed him the innumerable stars in the sky and grains of sand on the ground to cement that vision of the promise in his head. It followed him day and night. What did Abraham see by day? Sand. What did he see by night? Stars. It was as if he couldn't escape God's promise. Everywhere he turned he was reminded of his future; and that built his faith. As you move into the Motivation step, you will get excited about the direction your life is taking. You will begin to see the fog clear and gain energy and sanity back in your life. But to keep moving forward you've got to know where you're headed and build up your faith to get there.

The E ⇢ R Formula

It's difficult to move forward if you are dragging excuses along with you. We need to kick those bad boys to the curb right now. For years, I used my kids as an excuse for why I was so exhausted and overwhelmed all the time. They were my "out," and if I could blame it on the kids, I was free from personal responsibility to do anything about it. I could stay in my fog. Even though I hated the fog, doing anything about it seemed impossible. To protect myself, I just passed it off as my modus operandi.

It's a lesson you learn that first day you fake that you're sick so your mom will write you an excuse and you don't have to turn in that science project you didn't finish (or am I the only one who did that?). We learn early that if you have a good enough excuse, you're exempt from responsibility. Unfortunately, what feels comforting at the outset eventually leads to destruction. Excuses will keep you weak and tired. Excuses prevent you from realizing your potential. Excuses keep you stuck in a fog when God created you to shine with brilliance. And for the most part, excuses are just lies. They are lies we create to protect us from a truth we don't want to face. *Ouch!*

No matter how tangible your vision, if you still have excuses clinging to your feet, you won't be able to move forward. It's time to uncover any excuses in your life and use them to fuel your forward motion. We do that through a simple process called the E → R Formula.

First, uncover any excuses you find yourself using. Here's a hint: If you are rationalizing why you cannot perform better in life (build your business, clean your house, raise your kids, manage money, lose weight, get healthy, etc), your "why" is probably an excuse. For example, I used the kids as an excuse for why I was so exhausted and overwhelmed. Applying this formula, I turned my excuse (my E) into my reason (my R). Instead of playing the message in my head that my kids make me exhausted and overwhelmed, I replaced it with the message "I am an energetic and focused mom so I can raise my children with excellence." Instead of my kids being an excuse for being tired, they became my reason for being energetic. Take some time to write down any excuses you may be playing in your head (sometimes you gotta go deep), then craft them into your reasons for moving forward.

Karen, one of the moms inside Mom Mastery University, struggled big time with paper clutter. Bills were stacked up and forms needed to be filled out. She went through the Mom Mastery Method and realize her "E" was "I have too much paperwork stacked up and I don't have the time to sort it all out." When she applied the E ➤ R Formula, she changed her "E" to this new "R": My time and my emotions are valuable, so I spend a little bit of time each day to open and sort papers daily so I don't have the stress of clutter and disorganization." Within just a few weeks the stacks were gone and Karen had a whole new level of peace, in her mind and her home.

"I am a restored mom! Months ago, I lost control and almost fatally injured one of our kids. It was out of anger. I knew I needed to get better. I was trying, but failing. I told my mom I wanted to quit my job. She has you can't just walk away from being a mom. I wanted to quit because I will do anything to protect my kids, even from myself. No one knew how bad it was getting. Mom Mastery University has completely

changed me. I love my job! My mindset is great. My husband is thankful for MMU, as am I. If I can conquer the anger, I can conquer all. I was losing control but it's over now. So much goodness! So many blessings! I hardly recognize the mom that I once was."

—Aleisha W.

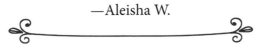

And as you begin to replace your excuses with reasons, your mind will immediately begin to move toward the "how." Believe me, I know how a mom's mind works. We jump to Bob the Builder mode and try to piece everything together. Chill on the "how." This is your time to discover your reasons and establish your "whys". Let God be in charge of the how. He already has a million ways to establish the immense promise over your life. That's not your job. Your job is to come up with the "whys." If you have a strong enough "why," the "how" will take care of itself. Because you don't need to know "how" as long as you know "Who." And I'm pretty sure I couldn't have fit more interrogative words into a paragraph if I tried.

As you give yourself grace on the "how" part, also give yourself grace over your excuses. Remember, this entire program is guilt-free. As you uncover excuses, don't beat yourself up over them. Forgive yourself, love yourself, and use those "whys" to create your vision for a better future. Shake off them shackles, Mama. And let's get to gettin'!

Eiffel Tower or Bust!

For years, my daughter and I wanted to go to Paris. I had dreamed about it, thought about it, and even bought home décor items with Paris stuff on them. Yep, that's me—the woman in the Walmart aisle with the Eiffel Tower throw pillow and the T-shirt that says, "C'est La Vie." As I learned about the power of vision, I realized that dream of going to Paris would stay at Walmart if I didn't take action toward it. So, I did.

I found a beautiful picture of the Eiffel Tower online and printed it out on card stock. Did you catch that? Card stock, Baby. This woman ain't playin'! I cut it out and taped it to my fridge. Every day, when I opened that fridge, I would see that picture of the Eiffel Tower and say, "I am so excited about going to Paris!"

Did I have a way to go to Paris? *No!*
Did I have the money to get there? *No!*
Had I ever traveled that far before? *No!*

The odds were slim, but my vision was big. And never bet against a mom with a big vision. Because that's all God needs—your vision. With it, He can do miracles. Without it, you perish. Perish or Paris? I'll take Paris!

As another act of boldness, I started a savings account to go to Paris. I remember the day it hit three digits—PAR-TAY! I know $140 is a fraction of the cost of a trip to Paris, but it was a start. The money grew slowly, but it grew. And as it grew, so did my faith.

One day, I got a notice in my email that one of my dear friends in ministry, Terri Savelle Foy, was planning an outreach to Paris. Paris! My heart did a couple of flip-flops in my chest and I immediately responded with "Yes! My daughter and I definitely want to be included in this trip!" It was only after I replied that I decided to click through and read the information about the trip. It would cost several thousand dollars each, not including airline tickets. Suddenly, my triple-digit savings account didn't look so impressive against the five-figure total cost. I started getting hot flashes, and I wasn't even menopausal. My flip-flop stomach turned into genuine nausea. *Oh, dear Lord Jesus, what had I just done?*

It was several months away, so I would have time to save up money. But at the rate I was going, it would be years, not months. I turned to God's Word and put my faith into overdrive. If this Paris trip was going to happen, it was going to be God, not me. I began to say out loud every time I opened the fridge, "Thank You, God, that I'm going to Paris!" I began feeding my family more beans and rice so I could put more croissant money into the savings account. I even started playing French music around the house!

As the date drew closer, I was able to get a speaking gig that paid enough money to cover the airline tickets, so I bought them. Two tickets—one for me and one for my daughter. The trip was less than two months away, and I only had enough money for one of us to go, but I still bought two tickets. And they were nonrefundable. When the worry and nausea would creep up, I would shove it down with God's Word.

God richly gives me all things to enjoy (1 Timothy 6:17.)
I delight myself in the Lord and He gives me the
desires of my heart (Psalm 37:4).
Nothing is impossible for me (Matthew 17:20).

It was just weeks away and the money was due in. I had turned in enough to cover one of the trips, but that was it. The savings account was empty, and the plane tickets were bought. I tried not to panic, but Bob the Builder was taking over. I began to construct another plan. Maybe just my daughter could go, and I would just take a loss on the plane ticket. But as thoughts scrambled in my head, I realized that I had trained my heart all those months to keep believing. It was an act of sheer will to keep believing and speaking and believing and speaking, especially as I saw our travel day draw closer.

That was when I got the phone call. Terri's assistant was on the other line and had news for me. One of the women who had planned to go had to back out and wanted to gift her trip to someone else. She asked if I would like to have that amount go toward covering the rest of our trip. I don't even know how I responded. I just know it was high-pitched and very, very loud. I was shaking as I hung up and then broke down in tears of joy. I'm convinced: Faith is the most powerful force on earth. And it all begins with a vision.

What if I hadn't held out? What if I gave in to doubt? What if I had never taken the bold step to buy the tickets? I'm convinced of this: As we act with crazy boldness God comes through with ample provision. He's just waiting to see how serious we are and how far we're going to take it.

As my daughter and I were sipping café au laits and enjoying a basket of croissants, I realized that none of this would have ever happened if I did not first establish a vision. I also realized that when you're in Paris you should never wear a Walmart "C'est La Vie" shirt. Trust me on this.

Keep It Simple, Sweetie

Habakkuk 2:2 tells us to "Write the vision and engrave it so plainly upon tablets that everyone who passes may [be able to] read [it easily and quickly] as he hastens by" (AMPC). This is one area where many people get confused about creating a vision— we complicate it. But God knows how we work, and especially how moms work. We hasten. We hustle. One version of this verse even says, "as he runs." A mom's life is never still. But that's okay. Because dreams don't necessarily come true for the sitters. You can sit on your dreams your whole life and take them to the grave. Dreams are manifested by the runners, those who are willing to pick up their dreams and put them in motion. I know you're a runner. You're a hastener, a hustler, someone who's not afraid to break a sweat. You wouldn't have made it this far if you weren't. But one thing is vitally important.—

You gotta keep it simple.

That scripture even advises us to engrave it plainly. If any system is complicated to use, moms will not use it. One time I tried a diet program where I had to count calories and log in every item I ate. It lasted for two days. That's it. If it's too much work, we tend to freak out and fall off.

God doesn't want you falling off your vision, so he tells us to keep it simple and make it plain. Just dive into your heart for a while and spend some time dreaming. There is no right way or wrong way to dream. It's just a process of actively discovering what your heart desires. God says He wants to give you your heart's desires, but first, you need to realize what they are. It's sort of like going to a restaurant and just saying, "Can you feed me?" Well, of course they can. They specialize in that. But you've got to simplify the matter and get specific about what you want. Place your order!

God specializes in blessing His children, but we need to simplify the matter and stop floating around all over the place. Get specific and lay it out. Do you want to travel? Where do you want to go? What do you want to do? Do you want to prosper financially? How much money does that mean? Do you want to achieve a goal? What goal? The world is yours, so let's have some fun and dream!

Remember, God's promises are for anyone who will believe. Create that vision so you can get your faith moving in the right direction.

The Captain Trains the Crew

Your inner mom is executing whatever your outer mom has taught her. That's why we need to reeducate that woman on who she really is. Remember, everything you have lived, experienced, thought, and voiced throughout your life has trained your subconscious. Your conscious (the captain) has trained your subconscious (the crew) on what you expect in life and the crew is simply following orders.

With my dream of going to Paris, I had to consciously train my subconscious that I was going to Paris, I loved to travel, I had plenty of resources, and I possessed everything required for an international trip. Up to that point, I had trained my subconscious that I didn't have money to travel, it was impossible to go on a long trip like that, it was too confusing and intimidating to travel internationally, and all the other lies that protected me from God's Truth. And my subconscious made sure that it followed orders. A trip to Paris was impossible because I had taught my "inner mom" that it was impossible. You'll find that inner mom is extremely obedient. She will create circumstances and make choices that support your beliefs—whatever they may be.

I could have stayed in those limiting beliefs, but I decided to teach that inner mom something new and unlimited. And that began by creating a vision. Putting a vision in place is an essential step to transforming your mind, instead of remaining conformed to the pattern of this world (Romans 12:2). When you put that vision before you, you begin to weaken those playlists that say it's impossible, and you write a new song of possibility.

But you've got to take action by getting it out of your head and putting it on paper. Remember, you can't do belief battles in your head. You need to get the higher ground. And creating a physical vision gives you an advantage.

"A year ago, I was stressed, depressed, yelling at my kids. I was daily running around putting out fires. My marriage was struggling, and it took everything in me to get out of bed. I had no goals, no dreams, and I was just barely surviving. I knew God didn't intend for me to live like this, but I had no idea how to live out the life I knew He wanted for me ... until I found Mom Mastery University."

—Sara R.

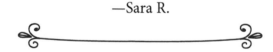

You can think about going to Paris all you want. You can dream of being debt-free or owning your home or running a 10K. But until you get that vision out of your head and into the physical realm, it doesn't really exist. Giving a physical manifestation to your dreams is the perfect way to begin the creation process. God didn't tell Adam and Eve, "Hey, you two, go sit down and let me multiply for you." He clearly said, "Be fruitful and multiply." God blessed them. He empowered them. And then He sent them out to keep the creation process going.

He does the same for us. He has blessed us and empowered us to create abundant lives, not to endure tough lives. Instead of sitting around waiting for God, we need to get to a place where we realize He's been waiting for us all along. We have so much creative power, but we need to act on it. Allowing your heart to dream, and then taking those dreams and putting them before you in visual form, brings them from the spiritual realm to the physical realm.

Even those dreams you have given up on, and those visions you thought you had missed out on—nothing is out of reach. You have the same resurrection power inside you that brought Jesus forth from the grave. Because nothing is impossible for God, nothing is impossible for you. Think big. Dream huge. Shatter the limits of your imagination. It's time to shake the dust off those dreams and call the buried desires from the tombs. Breathe life into your vision and let's create something amazing together!

⟨ Chapter 6: Vision Bored? ⟩

When I was a teenager, I worked in a small café in a country club. They did things old school. Henrietta was the head cook, and she taught me everything I know about pimento cheese and fried chicken. In the kitchen, a french fry slicer was mounted on the wall and underneath it was a bucket of water with a colander perched on the side. If a customer ordered french fries, Henrietta would grab a potato, stick it in the french fry cutter, pull the lever, and about 16 perfectly sliced French fries would fall into the bucket. She would lift them out with the colander and stick them in the deep fryer. Best. Fries. Ever.

Several years ago, I was in an antique store and saw an old metal french fry slicer. You know you've lived a long life when items you recall using find their way into antique stores! I bought the french fry slicer and brought it home. It's an odd-looking contraption, and despite all their guesses, no one in the family could tell me what it was used for. In fact, I don't use it for french fries. Instead, I display it in December, laying on its side with a couple of Christmas elves on it (it looks just like they're riding on an old metal sled!).

Vision boards are a whole lot like french fry slicers. They look really interesting, but no one really knows how to use them. We're going to solve that little predicament right now. Vision boards fit in perfectly with the Motivation step because you can use them as incentives to stay on your path of personal development. Perhaps you've tried vision boards before and never noticed any results.

Let me show you how to do it right, right now.

Walk-In Closet Déjà Vu

For several years, I've kept a vision board in my home. When I first started, my husband joked about my vision board being bigger than my office. He was right! I started my business out of a tiny room off the entrance of my home, and I shared that room with an old piano that was too big to move out. My vision board was too big to fit on any of the walls, so I propped it up along the side of the room. I had everything on there—the house I wanted, television opportunities, speaking engagements, books, even down to a picture of my dream closet. I covered it all!

Slowly but surely, the steps I took (the steps we are taking together in the Mom Mastery Method) started taking effect and yielding results. I took down the picture of the car I wanted because it was now in the garage. I took down the financial goal because it was in our savings account. New bigger, and bolder images began to find their way on to my vision board.

"I saw one of Hannah's videos and it gave me hope. I cried and laughed. That day became the first step in improving my life. I immediately started to implement the Mom Mastery Method and got amazing results. I'm enjoying life now! My family is drawn to me because of the positive energy that I now emit. I'm able to laugh and have fun with my kids. We

play regularly and 'yes' is said more often. My husband loves the new and improved me. I can't wait to see how awesome life will continue to become!"

—Heather J.

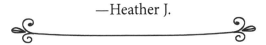

Then the craziest thing happened. Well, a lot of crazy things happen in my life. But this one in particular was like a scene from Inception. Through a strange turn of events, we found ourselves moving into a new home that was quadruple the size of our old home. It was a God thing (I'll tell you more about that later). The process from "Hey! I think we may be moving" to "Let's unpack some boxes" took less than three weeks. Mind-blowing! But as I was unpacking my clothes into my new closet, I got the strangest feeling of déjà vu. I tried to keep unpacking and sorting my clothes, but just couldn't shake that feeling. Finally, a random thought popped into my head.

I hustled downstairs to find my vision board in the piles of boxes and belongings from the old house. We couldn't pack it in a box because it was too big! I saw it propped up by the wall. I pushed the boxes aside and wriggled my vision board out. I glanced at it and what I saw made me gasp!

Years ago, I had come across a picture of a very unusual closet. I had never seen anything like it. It was a walk-in closet with shelves and drawers at the back, and glassed-in doors along both sides enclosing areas where you could hang your clothes. It was beautiful and so different. I cut out that picture and put it on my vision board. As I looked at that picture, with tears streaming down my cheeks, I realized it was exactly like the closet in which I was currently putting my clothes away. When I got specific with God, God got specific with me.

Vision boards work! But you've got to know how to work them.

Vision Boards: The Essential Guide

You would think a mom who is an expert at vision boards would teach her kids how to do it right, right? Wrong! One day, I had planned vision boards for a homeschooling activity. I got the corkboards, push pins, and scissors, and taught them all how important it was to establish a vision for your life. They brainstormed their goals and then found images that matched (Thanks, Google!). After all the printing, cutting, and pinning, they had completed their vision boards and my job was done. I went to prepare my acceptance speech for the Homeschooling Mom of the Year Award.

About two months later, I brought up the subject of vision boards. When I asked my daughter about hers, she confessed that she had no idea where it was.

"Didn't you put it in your room?" I asked.

"I thought so," she said, staring off into the distance as if her vision board was going to materialize on the living room sofa. I'm not sure how one goes about "losing" a vision board, but she had succeeded in doing so. The problem, though, wasn't that she had lost it. The real problem was that I had not taught her how to use it properly. A vision board is like a beautiful new car. It can sit in the garage and look pretty, or it can do what cars are meant to do—take you places. But you've got to use it. It's a tool, not a piece of art.

You have picture frames around your house, framing beautiful pictures of the past—wedding photos, family portraits, school pictures. But that's just it: They are all snapshots of the past. Think of vision boards as framed snapshots of your future. You are creating vision for your life and kicking off the creation process by putting the images in physical form. So, let's frame up your future!

#1—Pick Your Place

Just like Habakkuk 2:2 tells us, you need to put the vision before you. That means it's got to be where you will see it every single day. You need to retrain your "inner mom" to abandon her limiting beliefs. The more you expose yourself to bigger dreams, the easier it becomes to receive them. Remember, you can only possess what you truly allow yourself to receive. Continually seeing bigger and better realities in your life helps you to expand your subconscious to receive them.

So, pick a place in your home where you will see it every day. My vision board is on a wall in my office and my desk faces it. I look up from my desk, and there I am speaking to arenas full of people, traveling all over the world, expanding my business to a global market, and appearing on television. The more I see it, the more I can receive it.

"Before the summer started my 13-year-old daughter and I sat down and created a vision board for her. She has had some learning challenges and has struggled with feeling good about herself because of things others have said. By the time she starts back to school she will have accomplished all 3 of her main goals! Not only did she accomplish her BFG but she blew it out of the water!"

—Elizabeth J.

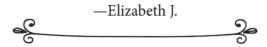

One of my dear friends, Debra George, has huge dreams of reaching the world for Christ. She got tired of trying to fit all her dreams and goals on a corkboard so now she covers an entire wall in her home! Like I said, she has huge dreams! Another one of my friends keeps hers in her closet where she sees it every time she gets dressed. Wherever you put yours, make sure you see it daily.

Also, it doesn't have to fit anyone's model. This is your vision board, so make it unique to you. You can put it on a corkboard, poster board, even the home screen of your phone or computer.

#2—Gather Your Supplies

You're going to need a computer and printer, scissors, pins, and some type of surface to pin them to. I know many people use glue, but that's only for artwork, not vision boards. A vision board is supposed to evolve with you; glue is only for committed relationships. That courtship with your image is temporary. Eventually, you will replace the image with the real deal, so you need to be able to take it off and switch it up. I've got an entire stack of pictures in my top desk drawer that I have taken off my vision board because I reached the goal. How cool is that? And you are going to experience the same thing!

Also, your vision may change over time. What once seemed appealing to you may no longer have the same pull on your heart. There was a time when I had prison ministries on my vision board, until I realized that God had called me toward a different field. I remember the day…

I was standing in the shower. It was right between shampoo and conditioner when I asked God, "God, please tell me my mission field." I have several friends in ministry. God calls some to drug and crime-infested inner cities, some to prison ministries, some to specific nations and cultures. So, I decided it was time for me to discover mine. Was it the prisons? The jungles? The inner city? "God, please tell me my mission field."

Before I could even squirt out the conditioner, the answer came:

"The kitchen table."

For a moment I thought I had misheard God. Maybe an angel was manning the phone lines and something got miscommunicated. *The kitchen table?*

Again, as clear as a bell—"The kitchen table."

It wasn't until months later when God showed me that my calling was for the home, and most importantly, the heart of the home. You'll often find moms in the kitchen. That's where the family gathers and lives are formed and transformed, where business is done and dreams are birthed. It's where forgiveness happens, and character is shaped. That's my mission field.

Allow yourself the grace to grow and change, and for some dreams to dwindle away so you can make room for bigger ones. And for heaven's sake, don't use glue.

#3—Start Dreaming

Before you start Googling "Fiji vacation images" take time to just let yourself dream. I know. You don't have time. I got you. May I suggest just carving out 30 minutes to an hour? If you have to lock yourself in the bathroom, that's cool. Pour yourself a cup of coffee, light a candle (especially helpful if you're locking yourself in the bathroom) and grab a notebook and pen. Now take a deep breath, and dream.

Divide your paper into six categories:

Faith – relationship with God
Family – marriage and parenting
Fortress – home maintenance
Finances – money management
Fitness – health and wellness
Freedom – personal development

Of course, you don't have to do all seven. This just serves as a basic framework. If you're a single mom, you can replace marriage with a vision for that amazing man who's coming into your life. As you come across each category, write down any and all dreams that come to mind.

At first, you may want to think small because you're still stuck in the "how" stage. Remember that is NOT your job. The Spirit of God within you already knows exactly how to make it happen and is more than capable of creating it. Your job is to communicate with the dreamer inside and let her come out to play. Just start writing. That's it. Let your imagination travel from one category to the next and put pen to paper.

"Before Mom Mastery University, I hadn't dreamed or had a vision since my wedding. I felt like I had forgotten how.

But that's all changed now! I'm no longer on medication, I've been sober for 6 weeks, I'm learning how to love more, and better, how to take care of myself, and be a steward of all the blessings God has given me."

—Jennifer G.

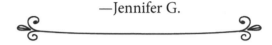

Now, I know that's a lot of categories. Many success coaches will suggest that if you have more than three goals, you won't be able to accomplish them because you won't be able to focus. Evidently, those success coaches never worked with moms. Moms, as MVPs, are required to focus on multiple variables at once. You know what happens when you pull all your focus in one direction, right? Everything else falls to pieces! Ever been there? You want to finish that scrapbooking project you started, but after a couple of days the laundry is backed up and the entire family is eating Honey Bunches of Oats for dinner. We spin a lot of plates. That's what we do. We can't sacrifice the plates, so we get super strategic with our spinning.

Let's think expansive. When Jesus told us in John 10:10 that He came that we "may have and enjoy life, and have it in abundance (to the full, till it overflows)" (AMPC), he wasn't being category-specific. That's a problem a lot of moms have, and it directly ties in to that scarcity mentality. We believe the lie that if we excel in one area, the others will falter. If you are brilliant in business, then you must be a lousy mom. If you are the fittest girl at the gym, then you must be a horrible homemaker. We do this because it feels safe. It's an excuse to explain why we are living beneath the calling placed on your lives. But if we believe that lie, then we have sabotaged ourselves from the outset.

In *Five Foot Two*, the documentary on Lady Gaga, she reveals a perfect picture of this self-sabotaging life: "My love life has just imploded. I sold 10 million (records) and lost Matt. I sold 30 million and lost Luke. I did a movie and lose Taylor. It's like a turnover." Evidently, her "inner Gaga" believes that if one area of her life succeeds, then another must suffer in order to even things out.

It's a lie that many women believe. If we achieve success in one area, then something kicks off within us and tells us that we don't deserve it, so we begin subconsciously ruining other areas of our lives. But when God gives something, He gives it in completion. He doesn't have to categorize anything, He says, "I am" and He doesn't have to follow it with anything specific. Basically, it's "You got a need? I'm your Man! I do it all."

Let go of the lie that success has to be categorized. God is enough to cover every single thing you touch. According to Deuteronomy 15:10 we can claim the truth that everything we put our hand to will prosper. That's everything, so start putting your hand to it—with boldness and confidence that you have all of heaven backing you up.

And give yourself permission to dream big. When I was helping a friend create a vision board, we started going through the categories: "So, in the area of money, what would you love to accomplish?"

I asked.

"Well," she paused. "I guess I'd like to be able to pay my bills."

"That's it?" I asked incredulously. "That's the big dream for your finances?"

"I mean," she stammered. "I'd like to be rich."

"Okay," I replied. "You're getting better."

"But, wait!" she blurted out, "Am I allowed to say that?"

For too long, society has taught us to play small. God wants to do something huge with your life. Not just for your benefit, but for the benefit of His kingdom. By living a crazy blessed life, you are just a walking, talking billboard of what God wants to do for His kids. Playing small is a disservice to God. You're here for more than just your needs. You're here to bring about God's kingdom, and that goes a lot further than just paying your bills.

#4—Get Your Pics

After you have scribbled out your entire dream future, it's time to warm up that printer. Sure, you could leave your goals and dreams written out on paper, but something amazing happens when you capture them in images—you start speaking your mind's native language.

There's a reason I put a picture of the Eiffel Tower on my fridge and not the word, "Paris." Your mind thinks in images, not words. If I mention the word "giraffe," you see a giraffe in your head. You don't see the word, "giraffe" spelled out. You see the orange patterned animal with a long neck and long legs. Because your mind thinks in images, the best way to establish a vision for your life is exactly that—in images. As you search for the images that encompass your dreams, make sure you keep the following guidelines in mind:

- Put yourself in the picture. Try to find an image that captures what it would look or feel like when you accomplish that goal. For example, if you want a fit body, then get a shot from behind, or a picture from the neck down so you can more easily imagine that it is your body. If you want to be a public speaker, get an image of what it would look like from the stage, not the audience.
- Get images with emotion. Sometimes we don't even know why one picture speaks to us more than another one, but honor that tugging.
- Don't sweat it. Sometimes you can't find the exact picture you want. That's okay. Just get an image that communicates your desire. For example, if you want a house on the water, but can't find the perfect one, just get a picture of a beautiful sunset on the water, so you can imagine yourself sitting outside your home, soaking it in.
- Specifics are good. God loves it when we are very clear on our dreams. One time, I had a picture of a man and a woman biking together on an island in another country. It captured

what I wanted in my marriage and family—adventures together. I was invited to go to Scotland to lead a conference and I brought my family along with me. As a special treat, one of the families at the church had planned to take us to the nearby island of Cumbrae and go biking around it. It was not something I would have ever organized, but I put the dream out there and God just showed up. Of course, we got a picture taken of Blair and me on our bikes, and it's almost identical to the one that was on my board. Yep, another picture made it to my desk drawer!

- Capture the ombre effect. Just like colors gradually fading from light to dark, give your vision board this same feel. I call it the ombre effect. I like to put those goals that I feel are within reach near the top of the board, and the huge dreams closer to the bottom. That way, I can progressively move them up the board.

#5—Experience It

This is the clincher. It's a vital step and the one most people leave out (which is why you get to a point where they don't even know where their vision boards are). They make it and forget it. If you let that happen, you just wasted a craft activity. You could have made a Chatbook in that time.

"It's happening! I attended a conference for women and never dreamt that a year later I would attend this conference as a

SPEAKER!!! I can hardly wait to take that item off my vision board and put it into my harvest folder!"

—Lorene W.

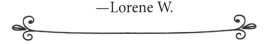

After you put up your vision board, make sure you pay it a visit, or two, or 12, every day. Don't just say you'll do it, make it a routine. Tie it into something you do daily. For example, if you have a cup of coffee in the morning, take those first sips with your vision board in front of you. It's your friend. Hang out together for a while. And make sure you do two things:

1. While you soak it in, practice stepping in to the final outcome. You may even want to set up a pattern where you touch each image as a way of anchoring it in your mind and then imagining what it feels like. What do you see? What do you hear? Get every sensory perception you can to wrap around this final outcome. For example, if you want to be a public speaker, what does the auditorium sound like? What do you see in the audience? Is the light so bright you can hardly make out faces? What does the mic feel like wrapped around your ear or clipped to your shirt? Get yourself in that place, and once you do, the next step is critical.

2. Make sure you shower the experience with gratitude. As you feel it, be thankful for it. I'm pretty sure if people ever saw my morning routines they would think I'm a lunatic. I'm touching a picture of Steve Harvey and saying, "Thank You, Father, that I have television appearances and speak with confidence

and clarity." I'm touching a picture of Lakewood Church and saying, "Thank You, Father, that I speak to thousands and communicate Your Word with excellence." Yep, they would have carted me off years ago.

Remember, your vision board is a tool. It ain't artwork. Put it to work.

#6—The Seed System

It's the last step in the vision board process, and definitely the most important—sowing! Next to my vision board I have envelopes that look like seed packets. I actually made little pockets, laminated them, and wrote on them:

FAITH SEEDS
"If you have faith as a mustard seed…
nothing will be impossible for you."
Matthew 17:20

One of the laws of God's kingdom is the law of sowing and reaping. If you want to reap anything in life, you've got to sow something toward it. Many people are frustrated with their lives. They want results, but nothing seems to be working. They're waiting for that magical day when the fields of their lives burst forth in an enchanted harvest of abundance. But there's one problem. That day will never come until they roll up their sleeves, get out there, and start planting seed. God is very clear on this:

"Do not be deceived *and* deluded *and* misled; God will not allow Himself to be sneered at (scorned, disdained, or mocked, by mere pretensions or professions, or by His precepts being set aside.) [He inevitably deludes himself who attempts to delude God.] For whatever a man sows, that and that only is what he will reap" (Galatians 6:7 AMPC).

In other words, don't kid yourself. If you think you can get something out of nothing, you're in for a huge disappointment. It's a law, just like gravity. Thinking you can reap where you haven't sown is like hoping you can jump off your roof and not go plummeting toward the ground. Good luck with that!

Your dream is valuable. It's worth something. You need to invest in it. What are you sowing toward your dream? I believe I will speak at conferences all over the world, so I put money toward supporting ministers who are doing that very thing. I believe I will transform the lives of moms all over the globe through faith-based coaching and therapy, so I invest in my growth and learning. Every single time I sow a seed, especially financial gifts toward His kingdom, I print out the receipt and stick that inside the pocket. That's seed money, and by law, it will reap a harvest.

I once got a vision for a conference for moms and stated planning it. However, when I looked at my bank account, I realized I did not have the funds to pay for it. Then I remembered something I heard a minister say, "When you find you don't have the money to support your dream, you're looking at your seed, not your supply." I realized when I looked at my bank account that I was looking at the seed to get my supply, not the supply itself. It was a huge act of faith to empty every single dollar (yes, every single dollar) out of that account and sow the entire amount toward a ministry I believed in, which was living out what I wanted to accomplish in my own life.

I planted that seed and then watered it with prayer and praise— thanking God that He was my source and He was coming through with the supply. I commanded that harvest to come in, in Jesus' name. And I kept it up for days, weeks, until that day I went to my computer and saw an email. It came from a ministry that heard about my conference and wanted to step in as a sponsor. Praise God! The supply came through! It wasn't toiling or effort or borrowing or scrimping. Instead of worry, it was praise. Instead of griping, it was gratitude. It was according to the system God set up from the beginning of time—sowing and reaping.

"The power of the vision board! I set the goal to wear a size 6 jeans and size small top by October 1st. I reached that goal already and it's only April 3rd! In January I was wearing size 10 and a women's medium. I am in awe!"

—Bethany L.

As you use your vision board to create your future, make sure you are continually sowing toward it. Are you believing for freedom from debt? How much are you putting toward it each month? Are you believing for that healthy body? How are you eating and staying fit every single day? Are you believing for your home business to take off? How much are you putting toward personal sales training? How much time are you setting aside to build it every day? Are you believing there's a book inside you? How much time do you spend writing?

And the most important sowing is the investment you are putting into God's kingdom. One of my mentors told me, "You get busy building God's house and He'll get busy building yours." Make sure you are tithing into God's kingdom. It's not that God needs the money; you need the blessing. You are believing for something big. You are building something huge. If you could do it alone, you wouldn't need God. But truthfully, it's too big for just you. Let God work things out on your behalf by plugging in to His system of sowing and reaping.

Keep It Up

I know it can get frustrating after a while. You make that vision board. You speak over it daily. You sow toward your dreams. And it seems like nothing is happening. Remember, you are sowing, and seed grows in dark places. Things are happening in the spiritual realm. You have started the process. Now let the process do its thing. It works. Every. Single. Time.

A farmer would never plant seed for his crops, then go out there a week later, throw down his pitchfork, and scream, "That does it! I did all this work and here's it's been seven whole days and I don't have a single ear of corn!" Trust the process. God set it up and it's working. Just keep it up.

Now, it's time to get laser-focused and start out on your Mission.

STEP THREE: MISSION

Chapter 7: Panic at the Disco

I was talking on the phone with my daughter as I was preparing everything to go to the grocery store. I had my meal plan, my wallet, my purse, and I was putting on my shoes when I stopped and looked around the kitchen.

"Oh, shoot!" I said.

"What's the problem?" she asked.

"I need to go grocery shopping and I can't find my phone," I replied.

"Mom," she said. "You're talking on it."

Just another example of how scattered moms can be. And, yes, this really did happen. I remember another time I couldn't find my phone, so I dug through my purse to find my phone so I could call it. You read that correctly. I was looking for my phone so I could call my phone and find it.

Another time, I was going through my bedtime routines on auto-pilot. My husband was sitting on the sofa and I grabbed his head and pulled it back so I could squirt some pink antibiotic in his mouth—the antibiotic that had been prescribed for our infant son. I had the dispenser in hand, ready to squirt, when he grabbed my arm and gave me "that look." It was the look I'm way too familiar with—the one that says, "Please tell me you're joking around because if not you need an intervention."

The scary thing? I'm pretty sure I'm not the only one who has done stuff like this. We moms are notorious for going around in a Mom Fog. So, how are we supposed to get focused, renew our energy, and rock our lives if we can't even manage simple things like locating a phone or figuring out which family member needs the meds?

Which Are You?

I'm sure you've been to a party with a disco ball spinning from the ceiling. It's fun! They're exciting, colorful, and all over the place! But sometimes the balls are spinning in our heads and it's not so much fun. You probably know that feeling all too well. You fall into bed at the end of the day and think to yourself, 'Well, one more day of getting nothing done.'

It takes the same amount of energy to power a disco ball as it does a laser beam, and a laser beam can cut through steel. As strange as this may sound, you don't need more time in your day, more strength in your body, or more clarity in your mind. That's what the world convinces us we need—more resources. But it's not resources that we lack, it's resourcefulness. You need to learn the strategies of how to effectively manage the power you already have. Too often, we spend our lives in disco ball mode and wonder why we're so exhausted and never get anything completed. When you learn laser strategies of goal setting and goal achieving, you will be able to cut through distraction, fatigue, and overwhelm like a boss.

Don't get me wrong. I don't want you to spend your life in work mode. I said at the outset this was going to be fun, right? Here's the deal with disco balls. You need them. You need bouts of unicorn frolicking and fairy glitter sprinkled into your life. You need the flannel pants, Ugg boots, and messy bun days. You need to blast the Backstreet Boys and sing until you're hoarse. I'm not anti-disco balls. If my family would let me, I would probably hang one in my living room.

But spinning every day eventually makes you nauseous. Being scattered drives us crazy; we often rationalize it by calling it "chill mode," when it becomes our daily existence. Instead of enjoying the flannel pants, we grow to resent them because they make us face a reality we would rather avoid—that we're wasting our days. Without structure and focus, you spend your time handling the urgent and unnecessary, and never get to the essential. By applying this step and learning key strategies of living out your Mission, you'll get the work done, so the fun can be fun (tweet that! #momfog). Unicorns and fairies always seem to appear more readily when the work is done, and the Backstreet Boys always sound better resonating in a clean house.

Mission Critical

Take my hand, and let's step out of the spin cycle into a whole new way of doing things, because the way you've been doing them just ain't working. Mission means you have goals; you have a directive. One of the definitions of the word "mission" is a specific task with which a person or a group is charged. Mama, you have a charge on your life, and it's a biggie. I don't have to tell you how important being a mom is; but I do need to give you a little reminder.

You are the lifeblood of that family. You are the spiritual thermostat. As goes the mom, goes the family. And if you want change—in your kids, your spouse, your situation—it starts with you. You are 500 times more powerful than you think you are. You have the power to change lives, break curses, confer blessing, destroy strongholds, and reign with dignity. Shake off the old lies that no longer serve you and step up to the mighty warrior God created you to be. You have a Mission. You've been charged. Now it's time to create your plan of attack.

That's what we're doing here—creating the plan of attack.

"When I joined Mom Mastery University, I was so overwhelmed as a mom and wife. I felt lost. The transformation I've had using the Mom Mastery Method is unbelievable! I love my life and am filled with so much joy! My marriage is better, my kids are amazing, and every year I am blessed more and more in all areas of my life. MMU has been the absolute best thing to happen to me and my family!
—Jill G.

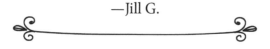

Sometimes you learn from people's success and sometimes you learn from their failure. In Genesis, Abraham gives us a glimpse of both. Abraham knew he had a huge promise over his life. He believed God when He said Abraham would be the father of nations. But, instead of doing things God's way, he decided to take matters into his own hands. (never a good idea.)

Instead of waiting on God to bring him a son through his wife, Sarah, he was suckered in to getting his wife's handmaiden pregnant in order to bring God's promise to pass. By the way, it was his wife that suckered him into it. I know, weird. Right? When God gives you a vision, He always supplies the provision, but sometimes when the promise looks impossible and the clock is ticking, you have a tendency to elbow God out of the cafeteria line and dish out your own servings. Only one problem here— God would have covered the cost. Now you're stuck with the bill. Abraham jumped the gun, did things his way, and paid the price.

But God is merciful, and He is all about the second chances. If you ever feel like you have screwed things up, then I've got good news for you. He's got you covered. I remember thinking I had to fix myself up before God could ever use me. I felt like some people were "blessed" and I was still stuck riding the short bus. Yes, I was that kid who was placed in special education. Just shows we're all special. But God's blessing is for everyone, and He doesn't play favorites. The only way Abraham could have messed up the promise is if he failed to trust God for second chances. He ended up plugging back in with his faith, and we can see the result:

"And so from this one man, and he as good as dead, came descendants as numerous as the stars in the sky and as countless as the sand on the seashore" Hebrews 11:12 (NIV).

Abraham was "as good as dead." In other words, the man was well beyond the years of bearing children. Not all his parts were in working order. But, fortunately, God doesn't look at our ability; He looks at our availability. Abraham made himself available, and he was able to get Sarah pregnant when he was over 100 years old! The dead has arisen! Even Hugh Hefner would be jealous! And if that's not enough, just to prove God does things in abundance, Abraham went on to have six more sons after that. Move over, Viagra, there's a new drug in town and it's called God's Word.

When it comes to establishing and achieving your goals, there is a worldly way and there is a kingdom way. Most people operate by a worldly perspective and that's why they abandon their New Year's resolutions before January is over. The reason you may be a "resolution reject" is that you have been trying to reach those goals from a worldly perspective. But, as always, God has a better way. Your Mission as a mom is critical, so let's create a plan of attack and do it right. The first step is to understand what you're working with. Let's take a look inside that "mom brain," shall we?

The Spotified Brain

Your brain is not engineered for your success. It is engineered for your survival. God knew what He was doing when He created your mom brain. As an MVP, you must be highly distracted. If you weren't, you wouldn't survive. Think about it—a mom is the caregiver of her family. This means she must be constantly on the alert for danger, risk, and opportunity. God created our minds to pick up on any change in our environment—a new sound, touch, sight. We pick up on these signals so we can be aware of potential threats.

Back in biblical times, an alert could be the rustling sound of a wild animal coming close to us, or a child tugging at our robes. Today, those alerts have multiplied at an ridiculous rate. We get a text alert, then a push notification about a 24-hour sale at Old Navy, then a call from a friend, followed by an Instagram message, all within 2.5 minutes. We can't even go to the bathroom without distraction, and usually, it's not a child knocking at the door. It's the video of a cat dancing that someone posted on Snapchat or the Facebook post of the top five foods that lead to belly fat. Distractions are coming at us from every direction. And we are responding to them just as God designed for us to respond.

"For most of my life, sleeping was difficult for me. My mind would be whirring with negative thoughts, worries, reruns of my mistakes and failures. Needless to say, I was not mentally, physically, or emotionally capable of doing a good job mothering my kids, which resulted in more guilt and feelings of failure. I started putting the Mom Mastery Method into practice. Before I even realized it, I was falling asleep with-

out worry and guilt. I had energy. I had mental clarity like never before as well as more control over my emotions. I also started losing weight without even trying. I praise God every single day. My life is totally different, and I have never had more energy, purpose, and hope."

—Bethany L.

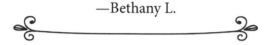

I remember one time when my husband and I went out on a date. We were driving to the restaurant, in a deep conversation, when we heard an alert go off on my phone. We both stopped talking and glanced at the phone. It was a notification coming from the app we use for grocery shopping, telling us we were close to the store. Wow! Two-person date going on here, and I don't think that app was invited along as a third wheel.

Digital media is a huge blessing, but a blessing can quickly become a curse if you don't know how to handle it. Take music, for example. I love that I can listen to any song I want any time I want. My oldest daughter and I share a love of music, and I'm so grateful for her. She's my go-to source for the latest tunes. If it weren't for her, I would still be blasting my Backstreet Boys jams (not that I don't do that on occasion). However, there is a huge problem with her music: She never listens to a song for longer than one minute. The song begins, and just when I start getting my groove on, she moves on to the next one. When it comes to music, she grazes. She doesn't dine. Apps like Spotify allow her to do that—any song you want, with a word or a touch. It's so easy, and so accessible.

In this day of immediate accessibility, we no longer have to dine on anything. We can watch six seconds of a video or listen to 20 seconds of music. We can Google any questions and get answers immediately. Awesome, right? But there's a problem. Our brains are fine-tuned to distraction, and modern media (and apps like Spotify) have allowed us to scratch that itch to our heart's content. Yep, our brains have become "spotified."

Yet, we're still trying to "muscle" our way into reaching our goals. Ain't. Gonna. Happen. Not with that method, anyway. We are highly-distracted people, and that's just the way it is. You don't have ADD and you're not doomed to a life of "Shiny Object Syndrome." There's nothing wrong with you. You just need to learn key strategies that work with the way you, as an MVP, are wired. And this, you can absolutely do. God would never put you in a position where He could not be your complete source for success. Put down the Adderall. You don't have to "add" anything to God's Word for it to work.

Method to the Madness

I never watch television. Like, never. We have a television and I have no idea how to turn it on. Seriously. We'll watch movies together, but television? Never. That's why when my husband came home from work on Monday and said, "Hey, I watched a couple of episodes of this show on Netflix. I think you may enjoy it. Wanna watch?" I was shocked. But then I thought, 'Aww, what the heck.'

That was our *"Stranger Things"* week. Sunday night around 1:45am we wrapped up the final episode of season 1.

Why am I sharing this with you? Because one thing that is driving you crazy is that you struggle to get stuff done. Distractions keep pulling you away. Makes you bananas, right? But if you have ever binge-watched a series on Netflix and you got to the last three episodes, you finished what you started, right? It's not that you can't finish what you start; it's that you don't have the motivation to do so.

We're going to change all that. But first you need to realize what is going on. See, I know that life. You're whirling around, juggling tons of stuff, and getting nothing done. There's that Go-Getter inside saying, "You can do this," and then there's Mrs. Pain in the Butt who says, "Epic fail, much?" You try to shake it and move on, but you don't have the strategies, and you completely lack the motivation. Why even try? It's all good, Mama. You've just created a pattern, and now we're going to stop it.

It's All About the Fruit

I'm so busy!

It's every mom's war cry! We should all speak in Scottish brogues, paint blue stripes on our faces, and scream it from the highlands. "Busy" has become the mom badge of honor, validating why we wake up in the morning and take that first sip of coffee. Ask almost any mom how she's doing, and she's practically obligated to use the word "busy" somewhere in her reply. If not, then what the heck is she doing with her life?

Now can I shock you? We were never meant to be busy. Busy is a four-letter word that causes strife and anxiety. You don't need to validate yourself to anyone. You're accountable to yourself and your Big Daddy God. That's it. And when you do things His way, you get a lot more done and have way more fun doing it.

In Genesis 1:28, God commanded his kids to "be fruitful and multiply." When I was a younger teen, I thought that was just his command to have sex. I imagined God setting the mood with some candlelight and the soft crooning of Marvin Gaye in the background. Nope. He wasn't limiting it to that kind of "gettin' busy." He was talking about multiplying in every area of our lives—our health, finances, homes, emotions, relationships—everything. God was talking about operating in that blessing He put upon us to prosper.

God created us in His image. And as if that wasn't enough, He took it a step further and did something even more awesome. He blessed us with the power and authority to operate as He operates on this earth. God would never tell us to prosper without giving us the ability to do so. When He says, "Go! Create! Prosper!" we just say, "Yessir!" and get to work doing it. But there are two ways to get to work—we can toil and stress out trying to get results in our lives, or we can operate in the blessing God placed upon us to prosper. Hint: His way is so much better.

That same command to "be fruitful and multiply" that He gave to Adam and, He also gave to Noah, Abraham, Isaac, Jacob, Joseph, and on down the line. Now it's your turn. He's giving that same command to you as well. Why does He want you to be fruitful? So He can bless you! God truly does desire for you to prosper in every area of your life.

> *"Let the Lord be magnified, Who takes pleasure*
> *in the prosperity of His servant"*
> (Psalm 35:27 AMPC).

So many people have a warped perception of God. They think He's "out to get 'em." If they make one wrong move, He's waiting to bop them on the head! No ma'am! Not our God! His love and mercy know no end. God takes pleasure in seeing you rise up and prosper. It's like the way we feel when we see our kids rise up in their greatness, operate in their potential, and become all they were created to be. God sees the incredible potential inside you. You have the Spirit of the Most High God within you. You have the power to command and create. You have the power to change your life and change the world. You even have power over all the powers of the enemy (Luke 10:19). Get that? Hell is intimidated by you! So, get this in your head once and for all—God wants you to prosper!

The second thing you need to fully grasp is that God has given you the power and authority to prosper. It's not about sweating and straining to squeeze out a few drops of juice from your life. It's about sowing seed and having a continual supply of juice, every day in every season. God has supplied a way for you to prosper and it's in His Word. When we do things His way, it works. We don't even have to understand how it works, but we have faith that it does every time.

"I have to share how much Mom Mastery University has changed my own personal life. Today, I confess I rode the shopping cart out of the grocery store. If you heard someone laughing all the way to the car, yep, that was me! I shouted for joy when the guy behind the deli counter called my number, and this started a chain reaction of 'Marco' and 'Polo' shouts all throughout the store. Yep, it's contagious. And I got to play 'catch the fruit in the bad' with my son in the produce aisle! Hannah has taught me so much about motherhood and best of all I'm finally learning to have FUN with my family!"

—Pamela E.

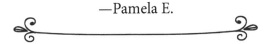

The reason you may be exhausted is that you're desperately trying to squeeze the fruit instead of reaping the harvest. The world's way is hard. You have to figure it out on your own. You get a problem and you turn to your friends, websites, Google, meds, whatever will pacify the situation until another symptom appears. The deeper issue is that you still think it's all up to you, and the struggle continues.

When you do things God's way, it's easy.

I need to state that again: When you do things God's way, it's easy.

If you have a problem with that statement, then it reveals the degree to which you've been trained by this world that life should be hard. Nope, not really. And if you have a problem with that, don't take it up with me. Take it up with Jesus. He said:

"Take my yoke upon you and learn of Me, for I am gentle (meek) and humble (lowly) in heart, and you will find rest (relief and ease and refreshment and recreation and blessed quiet) for your souls. For my yoke is wholesome (useful, good—not harsh, hard, sharp, or pressing, but comfortable, gracious, and pleasant), and My burden is light *and* easy to be borne" (Matthew 11:29-30 AMPC).

Check out that word in there—*recreation*. We have a tendency, as moms, to see recreation as hanging out on the playground or going on a Mediterranean cruise. Recreation means you are re-creating yourself. That's the root of the Mom Mastery Method—recreating yourself to get in line with God's design for your life. You can do things the world's way and end up stressed out, exhausted, and overwhelmed for the rest of your life. Or you can plug into His Word, rest in it, and get the results you want.

Busy Bee Syndrome

First, why are you so busy? You may answer, "I have so much to do," but perhaps it goes a little deeper. This part is where we both take a deep breath, hold hands, and look deep into each other's eyes. Ready? Being "busy" usually is more of an ego thing than a scheduling thing. (Squeeze my hands. It's okay). Sometimes, as moms, we don't value our career as highly as we should. We feel like we're stuck in a role that is a waste of our abilities, and is completely unrewarding. We know we could make it more than it is, but we feel like failures so often that it's not really worth our time and effort to do anything about it (Learned Helplessness). To compensate for our own inadequacies and feelings of insignificance, we resort to being busy.

'If I'm busy,' our inner mom thinks, 'then I must be doing this whole mom thing as best as I can. Look how needed I am!

It's the Busy Bee Syndrome, and it occurs when we have the wrong mindset. We buzz and buzz around all the fruit trees, but we harvest nothing (honey doesn't count). Remember, you are meant to be continually harvesting in life, not desperately trying to squeeze the fruit for a drop of juice here and there.

"[Most] blessed is the man who believes in, trusts in, *and* relies on the Lord, and whose hope and confidence the Lord is. For he shall be like a tree planted by the waters that spreads out its roots by the river; and it shall not see *and* fear when heat comes; but its leaf shall be green. It shall not be anxious *and* full of care in the year of drought, nor shall it cease yielding fruit" (Jeremiah 17:7-8 AMPC).

When we do things God's way, we are continually prospering and yielding fruit—in every season. We don't need to hustle, and we don't need to chase blessings. Blessings chase after us!

We were born to bear fruit in this life, to prosper, to multiply! It's inside you. You just need to know how to dig in and bring it out. It's success from the inside-out, the way God intended it. Busy makes you tired. Being fruitful makes you inspired.

The Killer Bee

When I was younger, I was a spelling bee champ. Not to brag, but I always won first place in every spelling bee at my school, until the day my stellar record came to a screeching halt. It was my turn and the teacher called out the word "*quench*."

'Seriously? Quench?' I thought. 'C'mon, lady, don't insult me. That's stupid easy.'

I immediately spoke up, "Q, U, E, ..."

"Incorrect," she said.

"No," I protested. "That's right," I responded. That word was ridiculously easy. She was the one who was wrong, not me.

"Hannah, that was incorrect," she demanded. "Take your seat."

My jaw dropped. I stomped my foot in protest and walked over to my desk. Immediately, I began plotting how I was going to destroy her, her car, her family, her home, and seek world domination so she would be sorry she made me take a seat. I knew I was right! She went to the next person.

"Gary, your turn," she said. "Spell the word, 'quench.'"

"Quench," said Gary, looking over at me with a smug face that I desperately wanted to shove my fist into. "Q, U, E, N, C, H, … quench."

That was when I realized my error. I had not said the word before beginning to spell it. I knew how to spell it but screwed up the procedure of the spelling bee. You're supposed to pronounce the word, spell it, then pronounce it again. I regretted my oversight but was still secretly plotting out that whole world domination thing.

Killer Bee Syndrome is when you have the wrong process. It's not that you don't know how to set goals and fulfill your Mission. Within you is everything you ever need—the wisdom of God, the Word of God, the Spirit of God. You've just been doing it the world's way, which is backward, hard, and counter to everything "mom" about you. Setting goals and achieving them is not hard, you just have to do it the right way. You've been the Busy Bee, and you've suffered through a few Killer Bees in your years, but now it's time to BEE the Master Mom. Together we are going to set goals you can accomplish. You're on a Mission, Mama. Let's do this.

Chapter 8: Your *Inner Mom* Goals

If you search "SMART goals," you'll find out that this is a popular acronym for setting goals. According to this advice, you need to set goals that are Smart, Measurable, Achievable, Results-focused, and Time-bound.

Perfect. If you're an SCP (Singular Constant Professional). There is a lot of wisdom here, but here's the deal with moms. We can set SMART goals all day, but we can't always execute them. And when we fall short of our goals, guess what happens? The guilt settles in on top of the overwhelm, and now we have no incentive at all to keep going. Mom Fatigue Syndrome, anyone?

Let's switch things up a bit. Instead of conforming ourselves to the way the world operates, let's dance to a new tune. Toss the SMART goals out the window and let's create something that works with moms and the crazy lives we lead. Trying to change the results in your life without changing the "inner mom" who created those results is hard work. It's toil, pressure, and counter-intuitive. Instead of SMART goals, which are designed to work from the outside in, let's create INNER MOM goals and work from the inside-out.

I is for I

Your goals are YOUR goals! And part of the "retraining" program is to make sure your inner mom knows that for sure. When you write down your goals, make them personal by putting the words

"I" and "me" in them. Remember, this is a system that works from the inside-out. The point of creating a Mission is not just to establish goals, but to stretch your subconscious to believe for bigger and better.

When you include the words "I" or "me" in your goals, your mind immediately internalizes them and begins to accept those statements as truth. When I pinned that picture of a walk-in closet to my vision board, I accompanied it with the goal, "My walk-in closet is beautiful and filled with exquisite treasures." It wasn't just any old walk-in closet, it was mine.

David understood this type of personalization when he spoke his goals to Goliath. He didn't just say, "Yo, Dude, you're going down." He told him exactly HOW it was going down and he made it personal.

"This day the Lord will deliver you into my hand, and I will smite you and cut off your head ..." (1 Samuel 17:46 AMPC).

I believe David wasn't just saying this to threaten Goliath. He was also saying this to build up his inner man and get his mind in a position to carry out this goal. Make it personal, put yourself in position, and you'll be able to whip anything that threatens to stand against you.

𝒩 is for Now

As long as your goals are in the future, they will stay that way.

Think about the resolutions you have made in the past:

I'm going to lose 20 pounds.
I'm going to stop yelling at my kids.
I'm going to save up $1,000.

These goals are already set up for failure because they are things that take place in the future. Remember, these are INNER MOM goals we're working on. You're not just pulling together a goal, you're educating that inner mom who is going to carry them out. On the deepest level you must receive these goals as truths that already exist so you can begin aligning yourself with that reality. Believe it's already done, and it will be a lot easier to make it happen in reality.

Think about it this way: When a farmer plants crops, he doesn't see them as fields of seeds, he sees them as fields of harvest. He has already calculated them into existence. His financial projections see them as already done. It's not a mystery that may or may not unfold. It's already written in the books. It's as good as done.

We are called to be imitators of God, and He is not the great "I will." He is the great "I am." Let's just follow the pattern He has already set. Instead of those previous goals, better versions may be:

I am 20 pounds lighter.
I speak with kindness to my children.
I have $1,000 in my savings account.

See the difference? It's as good as done. Convince yourself of that and watch these goals begin to manifest.

𝒩 is for Not Limited

Roald Dahl wrote the book *The BFG*, which was also made into a movie. It was one of my favorite books to read to my kids. It was about a Big Friendly Giant. He was a giant, but not your average kind of giant. He appeared threatening, but he was actually quite friendly. Something that seems overwhelming and scary, can often become one of your best friends. That's the way it is with goals. The ones that are the hardest to believe, are usually the ones God has assigned you to achieve.

But that's difficult for people to embrace, as the BFG clearly explains:

"The matter with human beans," the BFG went on, "is that they is absolutely refusing to believe in anything unless they is actually seeing it right in front of their own schnozzles." The BFG also said, "We is in Dream Country. This is where all dreams is beginning."

Welcome to the kingdom of God. This is Dream Country! If we only created goals that we could achieve on our own, we wouldn't need God. He wants to do the impossible through us.

According to Ephesians 3:20, God is "able to [carry out His purpose and] do superabundantly, far over *and* above all that we [dare] ask or think [infinitely beyond our highest prayers, desires, thoughts, hopes, or dreams]" (AMPC). As big as you are thinking, God is thinking bigger!

At least one of your goals needs to be that BFG goal, that desire that God has placed on your heart that is so big you can't even fathom it. You see no way you could ever achieve it, but you're going after it anyway. But here's the crazy thing. What starts out as impossible, eventually becomes improbable, and then one day it hits you—it's inevitable. The only difference between the huge achievers and everyone else is persistence. You set that BFG goal, get your plan together, then never, ever stop.

"I didn't even want to live anymore. Life was so overwhelming. It took handfuls of anxiety meds and antidepressants just to make it through the day, usually ending up with a bottle of wine to numb myself. I knew my kids deserved better. I was so ashamed of myself, and was even searching for ways to abandon my children. Getting plugged in to the Mom Mastery Method changed all that. My life is so joyful now and I'm finally being the mom my kids needed all along. I'm off all meds and now I'm helping moms live out their dreams as well."

—Bonnie C.

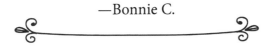

Remember, your job is not to figure out HOW. Your job is to

know WHO gave you the dream and trust Him in the fulfillment of it. You don't have to see it played out right in front of your own schnozzle. You do what you can; God will do what you cannot. So dream big! Throw the doors off your imagination and open yourself up to the miraculous. God wants to show up in a mighty way in your life, but you have to work with him.

The coolest thing about BFG goals is that they push the deepest parts of you to believe in more. I remember a mentor telling me, "I thought Denny's had a good steak until I went to Applebee's. Then I thought Applebee's had a good steak until I went to Ruth's Chris." As you supersize your dreams and goals, you supersize your ability to receive greater from God.

In Psalm 81:10, God tells us, "Open wide your mouth, and I will fill it." The question is not if God can fill you up, the question is how much you're going to let Him pour in.

ℰ is for Emotional

Although we think in images, language incites emotion in our spirits. When you create your goals, add as much positive and exciting language as possible. It helps to get your inner mom in line with the awesomeness of what God wants to do in your life. God's Word has an anointing over it to inspire us. Have you ever just come across a verse and it just totally transformed your outlook? That's how your goals need to be.

The reason we want to give these goals a positive language is that we are retraining our subconscious to get into agreement with God's abundant plans for our lives. If you believe it, you get excited about it, and if you get excited about it, you pull it to you that much faster! Check this out:

"'For I know the plans I have for you,' declares the Lord, 'plans to prosper you and not to harm you, plans to give you hope and a future'" (Jeremiah 29:11 NIV).

How cool is that? His plans are to prosper you! And when God does something, He does it in abundance, all the way. He doesn't leave any area out. So, get excited about His promise and let it come through in how you write your goals. Add emotional "feeling" words. For example, instead of "Drop three dress sizes" you would write, "I feel so trim and sexy fitting into my size 8 clothes!" Now, that sounds exciting, right? Instead of "Pay off $23,000 in debt," you may write, "I feel free and powerful paying off $23,000 in debt and being a lender, not a borrower."

By adding emotion to your goals, you are also putting yourself in the mental state of receiving them. Remember, God's work is done. Jesus said, "It is finished" when He died on the cross. He already has given you everything you need to live a life of abundance, power, freedom, and complete success. Stepping into faith and getting excited about the end goal does not move God to supply it. He's already done that. It moves us to a place where we can receive it. So, get excited about God's awesome plan for your life, and watch it come to pass.

$\mathcal{R}$ is for Reliant on God's Word

If you know anything about economics, you know that currency is only as good as what's backing it. Dollar bills are just little pieces of paper. It's not the dollar that's valuable. It's the institution backing it that carries the power to exchange it for goods.

Faith works the same way. Faith is the currency you use in the kingdom of God to achieve your goals and create an abundant life. In Matthew 17:20, Jesus says, "… If you have faith [that is living] like a grain of mustard seed, you can say to this mountain, Move from here to yonder place, and it will move; and nothing will be impossible to you" (AMPC). What's impossible? Nothing! But that's only if you put your faith to work. Faith is the most powerful force on earth, but it can't stand alone. It must be backed by God's Word.

If you don't rely on God's Word for your goals, then you will be tempted to doubt your Mission when things don't work out the way you planned for them to, or if the process is taking longer than you think it should. You'll begin to question your goals and the "what ifs" will begin to creep in. Faith is being certain that it will come to pass, but you've got to have something to back that faith, something you can rely on!

"… You have exalted above all else Your name and Your word and You have magnified Your word above all Your name!" (Psalm 138:2 AMPC).

Check it out! God's Word is so dependable, that God Himself even exalts His Word above His name! That means if He were to ever change His Word, He would have to change His name, too. And He ain't about to do that.

But what does that look like? What does it mean to be "reliant on God's Word?" It means to take your goals and see what God's Word says about them. Instead of forming your goals and sprinkling verses on them, dig deep and find out what God's "good, pleasing, and perfect will" is for you (Romans 12:2). Then form your goals around His truth. For example, instead of "Pay off $23,000 in debt," you would change this around to rely totally on God's Word for the manifestation: "According to Romans 13:8, I will pay off $23,000 and owe no man anything but love, in Jesus' name." Now, that goal has some punch to it!

"The Mom Mastery Method saved me! I felt overwhelmed, tired, angry ... I felt like I couldn't find joy in anything! Hannah helped me see a different way and my life is changing. So grateful!"

—Lacey Z.

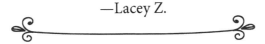

While you use God's Word, remember to use the name of Jesus, too. We have access to His name, which is above all names. When we speak in the name of Jesus, we are resting in the finished work that He did on the cross. We are saying, in effect, "This is already done and I believe it, I am moving toward it, and will not let doubt enter my mind."

"And I will do [I Myself will grant] whatever you ask in My name [as presenting all that I am], so that the Father may be glorified *and* extolled in (through) the Son. [Yes] I will grant [I Myself will do for you] whatever you shall ask in My Name [as presenting all that I am]" (John 14:13-14 AMPC).

See that? He'll do it. It's done. Jesus has given us access to His name so we can walk in His power. He even told us so, twice. Rely on His Word and the power of His name, and nothing can stand in your way.

𝓜 is for Measurable

God loves precision. Look how he created the world; everything in perfect detail. In Ephesians 5:1, we are called to be "imitators of God" so let's do that when we create our goals. If you want to make more money in your home business, how much more and how often? If you want to declutter your home, what areas, and by when? If you want to get in shape what does that mean? Running a 10k? A weekly yoga class? God loves it when we get specific with Him because it gives Him an opportunity to show off and do what He does best—bless His kids!

For an entire year, I had the goal, "I am so excited that 300 moms are at Mom Mastery Live!" I wrote it down daily and stuck a picture on my vision board. I was very specific with that number.

At our yearly conference, about 11 months after I wrote that goal, and kept writing that goal, I had no idea how many people had shown up. I only knew the room was full. On the way home, my daughter and I were talking about the event and how powerful it was. She then said, "We had 301 moms show up. Isn't that cool?"

I almost came to a complete stop right there on the highway.

"301 moms were there?" I asked.

"Yep," she said. "That was the final count."

I started crying, which isn't a good idea while driving. I was just amazed at how good God is, and how He honors the desires of our hearts. It was as if He was saying, "I'll see your 300 and raise you one."

God is so much fun to play with. The day after I got home, I put a brand-new picture on my vision board with a new goal: "I am so excited that 1000 moms are at Mom Mastery Live."

I saw His 301 and raised it 699.

When you back your goals with God's Word, you are backing them with a covenant, a promise between you and God signed in the blood of Jesus. Now that's trustworthy! When you speak His Word, claim His Word, and stand on His Word, then He goes to work bringing it about. In Jeremiah 1:12, He says, "... I am alert and active, watching over My word to perform it" (AMPC).

He's got a way to make it happen. You just need to keep believing, and relying 100 percent on God's Word.

O Is for Only Positives

Your mind only thinks in positives.
Hey, wait a minute, Hannah. You've been telling me that we need to get over negative playlists and limiting beliefs.

Okay, let me put it this way: Your mind cannot think in negatives. This is what I mean by that: Your mind (your deeper mind, the inner mom) cannot process words like "no" and "not." If your goal is, "I will not yell at my children," all your mind processes is, "yell at children." Remember how we see in images, not words? Even when you hear or see "not yell" you conjure up the image of yelling. That is where you draw your focus. And wherever your focus goes, energy flows. You will create that thing you're thinking about.

After Job had suffered total devastation, he said, "What I feared has come upon me." He was living in fear. He focused on it constantly, and he ushered it into existence. Faith and fear are the very same force, just operating in opposite directions. Faith is reaching into the supernatural realm and drawing out God's promises. Fear is reaching into the supernatural realm and creating destruction. Some call it the law of attraction; I prefer to call it the law of agreement. God wants to prosper you. Satan wants to destroy you. Check this out:

"The thief comes only in order to steal and kill and destroy. I came that they may have and enjoy life, and have it in abundance (to the full, till it overflows)" (John 10:10 AMPC).

The question is, who are you going to get into agreement with? God gives us the freedom to choose. He sets before us "life and death, the blessings and the curses: therefore choose life, that you and your descendants may live" (Deuteronomy 30:19 AMPC).

When you create your goals, use only positives so you can put those images into your mind and turn your focus in that direction. So instead of, "I will not yell at my children," how about this: "In Jesus' name, I will speak to my children with kindness and compassion because according to Proverbs 15:1 a soft answer turns away wrath." Sure, it's a bit longer, but you've put a powerful image in your mind, and that will hasten the manifestation. You've saved time in the long run!

$\mathcal{M}$ is for Multiple Categories

Get your vision board and glance through all the categories. God wants to bless you in all areas of life. Frequently, we only develop goals in the areas where we have the most "felt" need. For example, maybe marriage is never a struggle for you. You and your hubby coexist quite nicely. Where you feel the most pressing need, however, is in your homemaking. You want to get rid of the clutter and create a more welcoming, organized home. You will tend to only develop goals regarding your home—to declutter, get organized, clean up, etc. This is the typical pattern for most moms. But there's something wrong with that.

If you only focus on the areas where you are lacking, you may do so at the expense of those areas where you are naturally gifted. For example, if you focus solely on your home (where you feel the biggest need) you may pull away from focusing on your marriage (where you feel most fulfilled). And a sexless mama ain't a happy mama. We manage multiple variables, so we need multiple goals. Instead of growing in a singular area, it is imperative that we grow across the entire spectrum.

In Deuteronomy 28, God clearly tells us that His blessings are for every area of our lives—from our families, to our homes, to our careers, even to the food in our pantries. If His blessings are available for every area of our lives, then let's take advantage of that and excel in all of them!

The greatest part of this is that as you grow in the areas where you feel most fulfilled, you will have more energy and resources to improve those areas where you feel the biggest need. In the home/marriage example, if you establish goals such as enjoying more date nights, or making love more often, you will be feeding the area where you naturally gain enjoyment and fulfillment. This energizes you so you can tackle those other areas in life where you need the most improvement.

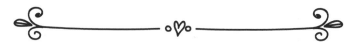

"Writing down the goals for my life as a done deal has given

me more hope and motivation than I have ever had. Just
writing that I had paid off my medical debts brought tears to
my eyes, and it's actually happening!"

—Denise W.

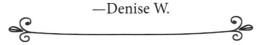

Also, you may overlook those areas where you are naturally more capable when you're continually inundated with life's demands. This is another reason why you often feel exhausted, overwhelmed, and stuck in that Mom Fog. You are trying to function on an empty tank. It's not that you're doing too much, but you're not doing enough in the areas where you have a natural God-given anointing.

For example, the home category comes easy for me. I don't struggle to keep things clean and organized. But when I get really busy with work, homeschooling, or volunteer work, I'll notice that I pull away from the home category and don't nurture that part of me. Although I maintain the home (because that comes naturally to me), I don't give myself time and space to just do activities that I enjoy—like beautifying a space or planting some flowers. You are a holistic woman, so your goals need to reflect that. When you write your goals down, remember to include all the categories: where you struggle and where you don't.

Creating goals in every area of your life may seem overwhelming, but keep in mind that goals in the areas where you are gifted don't seem like work. They're more of a process of "filling up the tank." Also, this is a system—the Mom Mastery Method—and

I'm going to show you how to kick butt with your goals so they're not toil, but instead a process of retraining your thought and lifestyle patterns to make those goals happen.

Should You Choose to Accept It

I'm sure you've heard of the *Mission Impossible* movies. In the beginning, it always explains a Mission by saying, "This is your mission, should you choose to accept it." God has given us all the privilege of living a life of focus, energy, abundance, and amazing productivity. He has placed an incredible calling on your life as a mom. But He's not going to force you into anything. You need to make the choice.

You're at that point. You're either on board or you've abandoned the program. I'm guessing since you're reading these words, you're in it to win it. I want you to know you're not alone. I'm backing you up with my prayers. I believe in you. And I know, beyond a shadow of a doubt, that God is going to lead you to places in your life that will utterly amaze you. He wants to delight you. His desire is to give you your desires. Trust Him and let's do this—together. It's time to move on to your Mindset. Things are about to get crazy up in here!

STEP FOUR: MINDSET

ᘒ Chapter 9: The Miracle in Your Mouth ᘒ

Have you ever seen the show, *The Walking Dead*? No need to watch it on television. You can see it everywhere you go, at the grocery store, the library, even at church. People are going about life with zero passion. The lights are on, but no one's home.

It's often the way you feel when you are struggling with Mom Fatigue Syndrome. You're just going about the day, making no progress and having no motivation to try. You're already three steps into the process of changing, and this is where it gets a tad uncomfortable.

So, Hannah, you thought it felt good up until now?

It's not that the process felt good. It's just that it didn't test your willingness to stand out and be different. Now, we're going to do that. As you move forward, it will feel weird. Faith always does at first. When all the fish are swimming along with the current and you're leaping and plodding and twerking your way upstream, it can feel awfully strange. "Call those things that are not as if they already are" (Romans 4:17) is just another way of saying, "Dat girl must be cray."

Just remember 2 Corinthians 5:13—"If it seems we are crazy, it is to bring glory to God …" (NLT). God's glory doesn't rest on those who are easily intimidated or self-conscious. It's that amazing place we enter into when we shed the superfluous, kick fear and reservations to the curb, and decide weird is worth it.

Ninety Minutes in Hell

"I'm going to a Bikram Yoga class tomorrow. Wanna come?"

I looked at the text for a whole seven seconds before I hastily replied, "Sure!"

I've learned to say "Yes" to things I normally would have said "No" to. I figure you'll always come out with one of two things—a great outcome or a great story. It was only after I replied to the text that I thought to Google what "Bikram Yoga" even was. That was so like me. Jump first. Google on the way down.

I found out that Bikram Yoga was another term for "90 minutes in hell." It's an hour and a half of twisting and stretching in a room that is heated to 105 degrees and 40 percent humidity. And I foolishly said I would go. I was dreading it, but had already committed. Reluctantly the next morning, I got dressed for yoga. I had to be strategic about it. I chose my dependable high-waisted, mid-thigh yoga shorts, the ones that doubled as sausage casings. They squeezed in all the extra fluff, and covered my slightly fleshy, heavily dimpled thighs. I selected an exercise bra, and then covered the entire get-up with a loose tank top. There. Now to work on the neck up.

I had to get that look that says, "I just tumbled out of bed and headed for the Bikram Yoga studio," and that look doesn't just happen naturally. I brushed my hair into a messy bun, which means I brushed it till it shone, then tousled it with my fingers to make it look a bit messed up before pulling it all on top of my head, fastening it, then strategically pulling out a few pieces to look even more careless. My bangs had to be perfectly coifed to the side, and then I lacquered the whole thing with hairspray.

Next, my face. I couldn't look like I was wearing makeup. However, since only a house fire would send me out of the house without it (and it would have to be life-threatening at that), I had to do something. I put concealer on all the imperfections—age spots, pimples, dark circles. Then I covered my face with tinted moisturizer (like makeup, but you can't tell). A touch of waterproof eyeliner, waterproof mascara, some powder, and I was ready to Bikram like a boss!

We arrived at the studio with my water bottle in hand and the matching yoga mat tucked under my arm. Hey, I'm not going looking like some amateur. I signed the waiver, which I should have read a little more carefully, then entered the studio. When I walked in, the heat hit me square in the face and almost drove me out. I didn't understand. I paid my electric company a lot of money to get rid of this stuff, and now I was walking right into it? And paying for it? I was convinced I had walked into the seventh layer of hell. I expected to see Beelzebub standing in the corner, passing out welcome fliers.

But it was too late now. I was stuck. We went through several cycles of breathing, opening and closing our arms. I breathe all the time. I never knew it could make you nauseous. Then came the stretching. I began to glow as sweat formed on my body. We were only 20 minutes in. Jesus, be my yoga mat. I needed help. Thirty minutes. Sweat was now trickling down my back. Forty minutes. Dear God, I was dripping on the floor. Was that sweat? Blood? Tears?

My shirt was literally soaked at this point, as I was trying to stand on one leg, with the other leg wrapped around it, and my arms wrapped around each other. If I lost my balance I would not have time to unwrap. I would be one solid pillar of tangled woman, crashing to the floor. Must. Maintain. Balance.

My carefully coifed bangs were now glued to my forehead and stuck to the layer of sweat that quickly went from glowing to gruesome. My face was a mixture of shades varying from red to deep purple, and I could clearly see the veins bulging at my temples, as well as on my legs. The makeup was long gone, and what was left of the mascara was just a black smudge under each eye, which helped to hide the dark circles.

At one point we had to stand up, spread our legs as wide as possible, and with our hands wrapped behind our calves, pull our heads down through our legs. When we did this maneuver, I caught a glimpse of my backside in the mirror. Oh, Lord, no! Was that a sweat line running down my butt crack? Say it ain't so!

Suddenly, something came over me. I'm a modest person by

nature. But the Bikram was kicking my butt. I grabbed my shirt and stripped the soaking wet thing off my body. I was coming apart, literally. I had finished off all my water 10 minutes earlier and now was pretty sure death was knocking at my door with its hot, fat, sweaty, little fist.

Sweat was now covering my yoga mat and pooling up in places. I rolled down the high-waisted shorts as low as they would go without making me look like a stripper, and pulled the mid-thigh portion up so they hit my underwear line. I didn't care at this point. I looked like I was doing yoga in a bikini. The cellulite below my butt was exposed for all the world to see. The stretch marks all over my abdomen? Check 'em out, Baby! The rolls around my torso? There they were, shimmering and forming sweat lines across my belly. I totally didn't care. All inhibition had dripped off me and landed on the yoga mat.

I then heard Satan—*I mean the yoga instructor*—say, "That was your last cycle, lie back, breathe, and enjoy the meditation. I'll be back with a cool towel for each of you."

Cool towel? I needed a puke bucket.

On the way out, she asked if I would like to get a membership. I believe I said something like, "Get thee behind me." There's a nice big vertical sweat line back there for your viewing enjoyment. That last hour and a half were as close to hell as I ever want to get.

Only Crazy People Talk to Themselves

Many people said "Yes" to Jesus for their "Get Out of Hell Pass." But God doesn't just want to give us abundant life in heaven. He wants us to live it here on earth, too! Jesus even said, "on earth as it is in heaven." People can be born-again citizens of heaven and live the most miserable, stinkin' lives imaginable here on earth. The Mom Mastery Method isn't just a cure for Mom Fatigue Syndrome. It's going to kick your life to a whole new level. It's going to bring some heavenly living here on earth, but you've got to be willing to be a little crazy. You've got to strip off the "what will people think" and shed all the insecurities. It's okay if it makes you sweat a little, just make sure you sweat off your inhibitions while you're at it.

"I suffered from chronic fatigue for years. This led to zero motivation and lots of overwhelm. I did not have the energy that other people seemed to have. I had lost joy and hope. After implementing the Mom Mastery Method, I found that I was joyful and energetic again. Not only did I have to tools to conquer my day, but I had the energy to do it. I now control my day instead of letting it control me!"

—Gerda G

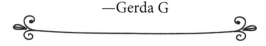

Yes, I'm going to ask you to step outside of your comfort zone, but that's where all the good living is. I found out in my Bikram

Yoga class that no one cared what I looked like. They didn't care that I had varicose veins, stretch marks, fat rolls, or even a sweaty butt crack. Get this in your head right now—NO ONE CARES. Everyone else is too busy caring about themselves. If you are going to make this method work, you cannot stay in your head. You've got to get it out of your head and put it in your mouth.

Now is when it gets crazy.

I've heard that people who talk to themselves are crazy. If that's true, then we must all be crazy because we all talk to ourselves, but not everyone does it by design. You're speaking over your life constantly, and usually, you're speaking what you have, not what you want. And whatever you say, you'll just keep getting more of it. In fact, your life is a sum total of the words you have spoken. You're a prophet; you just may not have realized it. You are constantly prophesying your future. Good or bad, you speak it into existence.

What would happen if we took that power to speak things into existence and used it on purpose to create the abundant life God designed for us to live? Now, we're talking! Yeah, it works. But sometimes it just feels foolish.

Before Abraham's encounter with God, his name was Abram. God renamed him, giving him a new identity. He gave him the name Abraham, which means "father of a multitude." Think about how Abraham felt when he introduced himself to people.

New Friend: Hi there! Haven't seen you around these parts. What's your name?

Abraham: Hi! The name's Abraham.

New Friend: Oh! Cool! Father of nations, huh? So, how many kids you got?

Abraham: None.

(Awkward silence while New Friend backs away slowly.)

New Friend (speaking to old friends): Y'all, there's a crazy dude in town.

The reason God changed Abraham's name is that He had to get him to see himself differently. He had to change his identity. And God knew the best way to change people's identities was to change how they speak of themselves. Abraham traveled around a lot, so he would constantly have to introduce himself to people. Over and over, he was hearing himself say that he was the father of multitudes. Eventually, the name (and the identity) stuck. He was able to accept it, and when he did, his life changed drastically. His identity didn't change his name. His name changed his identity.

"I had a lingering heaviness and thoughts of 'I can't do this.' Mom Mastery University has reminded me of the Truth and all the lies I've believed are now in the pit of hell. It doesn't mean they don't pop up anymore, it means I now know my defense to it and it's removed quickly. We can do life in abundance!"

—Shannon G.S.

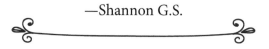

In the Mindset step, you are going to completely change how you speak of yourself, your life, your everything. It feels crazy at first, but we're stripping off all your reservations and plowing forward. You're not going to get this far and stop now. Not when your future hangs in the balance.

Half Isn't Whole

You wouldn't go to the grocery store with one shoe on and one shoe off, yet many moms are hobbling their way through life with only half the formula. In Revelations 12:11, God gives us a formula for how we are to overcome in life. It's our recipe for the abundant life that Jesus promised us:

"And they have overcome (conquered) him by means of the blood of the Lamb and by the utterance of their testimony …" (AMPC).

How do we overcome the enemy and create the life we were born to live? Two things—the blood of the Lamb, and the word of our testimony. Jesus shed His blood to rescue us from hell and give us an abundant life here on earth. But that's only one part of the formula. It's God's part, and His part is done. The other part is on us. We have to speak it into existence! God has done His part. We need to do ours. We need to get into agreement with His Word and speak it over our lives.

God doesn't want you living a halfway life. He wants you going all the way, "that you may be filled [through all your being] unto all the fullness of God [may have the richest measure of the divine Presence, and become a body wholly filled and flooded with God Himself]! (Ephesians 3:19 AMPC)

Hot diggity dog! I want that kind of life, don't you? To be wholly filled and flooded with God Himself! When God is flooding your life, there is no room for any lack, anxiety, fatigue, depression, pain, or exhaustion. God has done His part, now do yours. Speak up! Declare His Word over your life and watch the glory pour in and push the darkness out.

Affirm Foundation

I'm sure you've heard about "affirmations." Affirmations are just statements you say aloud to affirm the reality you want to experience. In the Mom Mastery Method, they are your goals, spoken out loud.

> *But can't I just post them in my bathroom*
> *and read them every day?*

Remember, success belongs to the people who are willing to look a little (or a lot) crazy. The people who don't care what people think, and do what they need to do to get where they want to get. If you want a life that is focused, productive, abundant, and joyful, you cannot skip this step.

"I used to say, 'I hate money!' Like it was a real deal hatred.

I hated that we needed it, that there was never enough of it.
I grew up with all negative talk of money. Over the past year
with Hannah this has changed SO MUCH!"

—Amanda S.

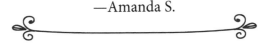

You listen to yourself more than any other person in the world. But more than that, you believe yourself more than anyone else. That means when you say something about yourself, your "inner mom" will believe it to be true and will do whatever she needs to do to make it a reality.

If you constantly say, "We never have enough money to make it to the end of the month," then your subconscious will make that a reality. Your subconscious is just obeying orders from what you have perceived and experienced on a conscious level. If you constantly say, "I am so exhausted," then guess what, you always will be. That inner mom will see to it!

If you want to change your life, you need to change your words. There's no getting around it. You can't wage war with thoughts. It's time to speak up. Your goals will do you no good at all if they remain goals. You give them life when you utter them. It's time to speak up.

At one time, you spoke the problem.

Now you're going to speak the promise.

At one time, you hid from the dark.

Now your words will bring forth light.

At one time, you lived by default.

Now you're going to rule by decree.

At one time, you ran from the storm.

Now you are becoming the storm.

Let's make some noise!

Chapter 10: Talk a Big Game

As children of God we have access to one of the most powerful weapons the world has ever known, and most people never consciously use it. It is the power of life and death (Proverbs 18:21), and it's all right there inside your mouth! You are speaking your life into existence with every word you say. So, be careful, little mouth, what you say.

God made us in His image and gave us the power and authority to operate as Him on this earth. When you speak here on earth you are using that creative power. You are reaching into the heavenly realm with your words and bringing that reality into your world. God has given all of us that power. He says we can "call those things that are not as if they already are." I truly believe when He tells us this; He is not just telling us to use our faith to speak of things as if they have already occurred so we can hasten them into physical manifestation. But He is also reminding us that we are living with a reality we have already spoken into existence—good or bad.

What we bind on earth is bound in heaven, and what we loose on earth is loosed in heaven (Matthew 18:18). We use words to bind and loose things here on earth so they can come into our lives from heaven. Want to loose energy and abundance in your life? Use your words. Want to bind anxiety and overwhelm? Use your words. This process of speaking things into existence is so important, God even started His bestseller with a perfect example for us to follow:

"The earth was without form and an empty waste, and darkness was upon the face of the very great deep. The Spirit of God was moving (hovering, brooding) over the face of the waters. And God said, Let there be light; and there was light" (Genesis 1:2-3 AMPC).

"I used to feel like such a failure because I had a hard time finishing anything. Projects would pile up half done, BUT then I embraced the Mom Mastery Method and changed my mindset and inner dialogue. I began to BELIEVE I am a finisher and I complete the tasks I set my had to. Everything changed!"

—Maggie G.

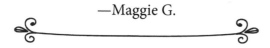

When you first started this program, you probably felt the weight of Mom Fatigue Syndrome—like your entire life was without form and an empty waste, every day just bleeding into the next with nothing to show for it. The very deep, your inner mom, was a dark place, full of limiting beliefs. I want you to understand that even in the middle of the darkness, the Spirit of God was hovering, moving, waiting. He's done His part. Remember the happy ending to your success story was already written the moment Jesus breathed out those words, "It is finished." He has been waiting for you to do your part.

Just speak the word.

Nothing would have changed if God had not spoken. But at His Word, the entire universe burst into existence. Just try to imagine what He can do in your life. He's just waiting on a word. But nothing will change until you speak something different.

Whatever You Say

I was skeptical at first. I started hearing a lot about this whole "speaking your faith" thing and finally decided to put it into practice. My oldest son, Kyler, had always struggled with his weight. We had tried diets, personal trainers, video programs, gym memberships, accountability partners—everything. Remember there are two ways to operate—man's way or God's way, earthly or heavenly, natural or supernatural. I had finally gotten to the end of my way and decided to let God have a shot (I wish that had been my first response!). For about two months when I would go for my daily walk, I would speak out this affirmation, along with several others: "Thank You, Father, that Kyler is a man of diligence and discipline. Thank You that he cares for your temple and honors his body, in Jesus' name!"

One morning, he woke up and declared, "Mama, I'm going to go to the gym today. Is that cool?"

"Sure!" I casually replied. Inside my heart was leaping for joy.

The next day he went again. And again. And again. Pretty soon, he was weighing his food and writing down everything he ate. In just a few weeks, we were at Target getting new clothes. People started using adjectives like, "trim," "ripped," and "daaaaang" to describe him. In less than three months he dropped 50 pounds. And I never once had to coax him to do it. God took over. He is the One Who changes hearts and minds. And as moms, we have authority over our families. I put that authority to use and "called those things that are not as if they already were." And they became. Hallelujah and pass the pre-workout drink!

It's time to take authority over your life and talk it up!

Since discovering the power of the spoken word, we have adopted a saying around our home—"Whatever You Say." It's a way to keep us all accountable for every single word that comes out of our mouths. And we use it all the time. But, be warned. If you decide to implement this around your house, everyone is fair game, even you.

"I'm coming down with a cold."
    Whatever you say!
"We're going to be late for church."
    Whatever you say!
"I'm so exhausted."
    Whatever you say!

One reason you are so overwhelmed and exhausted is that you keep telling yourself you are. Your inner mom is doing all she can to make your beliefs a reality. When you change your words, you change your Mindset; when you change your Mindset, your life will have no choice but to follow suit. Your reality is whatever you say.

Proclaim It!

Affirmations can often feel weak. Your mouth is saying one thing, but your mind is thinking something else. Instead of speaking affirmations, may I suggest speaking proclamations? There is so much more power there! The word "proclaim" is made up of two words—"pro" and "claim."

"Pro" is a Latin root meaning, "before, forward, beforehand, in advance."

"Claim" means "to demand by virtue of right or authority."

When you proclaim something, you are advancing the possession of something that is rightfully yours. If you want to claim it, you must proclaim it!

The Hear It/Speak It Formula

For this step, you are going to take the goals you created in every area of your life and turn them into proclamations you speak over yourself. You listen to yourself with more acuity and processing ability than you listen to anyone else. So, we're using this for your benefit. You will hear your goals and then speak your goals. It's the Hear It/Speak It Formula and it will supercharge your success.

#1: Take all the goals you wrote down from STEP THREE: MISSION. Make sure you followed all the directions so they are your INNER MOM goals.

#2: With your phone or some type of small, portable voice recorder, record yourself saying these goals. You can use Voice Memo for iPhone or Voice Recorder for Android. Record them using the following tips:

- Leave ample time between speaking the goals to repeat them back without being rushed.
- Say them in a positive, excited, happy voice!
- Continue as you need to. My Voice Memo lasts for almost 10 minutes!

#3: Schedule a time during the day that is 100% non-negotiable when you can run your recording, beginning to end. I listen to mine when I go on my daily walk (also helps me to remember to exercise). You may also want to listen on your way to work or when you are doing your hair and makeup for the day.

#4: When you run this recording, you will listen to yourself speaking your goal, then you will repeat it out loud. This is vital. It's the Hear It/Speak It Formula. You must hear yourself say it, then speak it back.

#5: When you say it out loud, make sure you imagine it clearly, see it vividly, and get excited about the finished product.

In Mark 11:23, Jesus tells us that "...whoever says to this mountain, Be lifted up and thrown into the sea! and does not doubt at all in his heart but believes that what he says will take place, it will be done for him" (AMPC).

Did you get that? It's not whatever he thinks, but whatever he says. The Hear It/Speak It Formula is how we take our faith and put it into action. When we hear it and speak it, our Mindset can transform so we can position ourselves to receive it.

Bubble Up and Boil Over

Now you know how to change your Mindset—with words! But words need to be activated. Words mean something different to everyone. For example, the words "almond butter" makes me happy. They makes me think of that delicious substance that I smother all over my apples and bananas. For my oldest daughter, Kelsey, who has a nut allergy, they bring up an entirely different emotion.

Words are vessels and they can carry a huge amount of power. When you fill them with positive emotion, it's like putting your faith into hyperdrive. As you speak your goals (your proclamations), conjure up the emotion that corresponds with each goal. For example, when you say "In Jesus' name I owe no man anything but love. I have paid $20,000 and am free of debt!" how do you feel? Excited? Free? Powerful? Charged? Put yourself in that state as if it is already done. Let your emotions correspond with your words.

"Mindset was a huge problem for me! I was too fat, too stupid, too lazy, too temperamental, etc. After some time in MMU, I started writing down promises in the Bible that spoke differently of me. 'I am beautifully and wonderfully made. I am loved. I am more precious than diamonds.' This chokes me up to even write because I remember a time when I truly believed that no one could ever seriously love me and it caused major issues in my marriage. Now I know how loved I am, I know my worth, I know that I am highly favored!"

—Akeisha D.

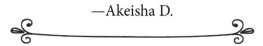

There are days when I've left the house on my morning walks feeling totally "meh." But by the time I speak all my proclamations aloud and have placed myself in that emotional state, I am positively over the moon by the time I get home. My neighbors have even seen me fist-pumping and stomp-walking on the street, which is probably why they call their children inside when they see me coming. Remember, you gotta be a little crazy. If you're worried about what the neighbors think, then maybe you need a new 'hood, or a new 'tude.

Remember that you are not necessarily after a goal, you are after how that goal makes you feel. And you have the power to create that feeling anytime you want. The key is gratitude. Be grateful for what you have and grateful for what you have yet to receive.

That gratitude will push aside every obstacle and make room for abundance to burst through.

The Wonder Twins

My youngest daughters are like twins. They act together, sing together, wear the same clothes, have their secret handshake, share the same room, even have their secret code words. When you see one of them, just wait a few seconds, and you'll see the other one. They're inseparable.

Did you know that faith has a wonder twin? It's a secret code hidden in the Bible—right there in Hebrews 6:12

"… behaving as do those who through faith (by their leaning of the entire personality on God in Christ in absolute trust and confidence in His power, wisdom, and goodness) and by practice of patient endurance and waiting are [now] inheriting the promises" (AMPC).

Let's make it a little simpler. Here's another version:

"… be imitators of those who through faith and patience inherit the promises" (RSV).

Or maybe this version:

"… Be like those who stay the course with committed faith and then get everything promised to them" (MSG).

Faith has a twin, and its name is Patience. When Faith and Patience get together, wonders never cease! This means you must believe it, speak it, and do not stop. That is committed faith. A commitment is for keeps. You don't turn away from it or get discouraged and give up. You'll have plenty of opportunities to get discouraged, but know that now and make a conscious decision that you will not veer off the path of faith.

Just Around That Next Bend

My son, Korben, and I love to ride bikes. Our neighborhood is pretty expansive and after a couple months, we still had not learned all the streets yet. We took a new road we had not traveled on and kept going, and going, and going. We puffed up the hills, and flew down them. Pretty soon, my thighs were burning and I didn't think I could take another hill. We saw the road rise up before us and Korben must have read my mind. Either that or my grunting and wheezing were louder than I realized.

"You want to turn around and go back?" he asked.

"Yes," I replied, in between breaths.

"We're going to have to do all those hills again," he remarked. Yeah, tell me something I don't know, like how to stop my thighs from cramping up.

Then I looked up and noticed there was a level area at the top of the hill with a stop sign. I'm a biggie for reaching goals and I'm always pushing myself to go further. He is, too. I raised him right. "Look up there," I said. "There's a stop sign. Why don't we just make it to that and turn around and go back?"

He didn't even reply but took off pumping his bike up the hill, with me following him. After about 15 seconds, I regretted the idea but kept going. I didn't want to have to get off the bike and push it, but my legs were about to give way and I felt like my heart was going to beat out of my chest. I looked up. Just a little bit more. I sucked it up, reached down deep, and kept pedaling. In my mind, I was in the Olympics, battling for the gold, with sinewy muscles bulging out of my Nike biking shorts. In real life, I was on an 18 degree incline in my neighborhood wearing Target leggings.

Finally, we made it to the stop sign. Before I could even catch my breath, I noticed something that made my heart leap for joy (or it could have been the cardio). The stop sign was right by the street that leads to our home. We had done a full circle! We didn't need to go back and do all those hills. We had arrived!

My son exclaimed, "We made it back!" I made a feeble attempt to reply but was still trying to catch my breath.

He then added, "Could you imagine if we could see ourselves on a map and had decided to turn around and go back?"

Persistence works. Every single time. About 98 percent of people don't really know how to put their faith to work with their words. Now you know. You've made it to the 2 percent. But what people don't know is there's a 2 percent of the 2 percent. About 98 percent of the people who learn the power of speaking their goals only do it until they grow weary of it or they become tired of the neighbors thinking they're crazy. Two percent keep going. With Faith and Patience, we inherit the promises. Just let the wonder twins do their thing.

"I have always heard that joy is a choice. But I always felt that it wasn't for me. After being in Mom Mastery University and saying daily proclamations, I now truly know that joy is a choice, and that anything is possible. I now am being published for the first time!"

—Michelle T.

When you imitate God and speak your hope into existence, you are doing the right thing. But that doesn't mean your old belief systems aren't going to rise up in protest now and then. You are transforming yourself and that takes time. You will constantly be tempted to stop the supernatural and pick up that old yoke that is pressing and difficult. Don't do it. Every word you utter is a seed, and seed grows in dark places. Things are happening in the spiritual realm. Your goals are trying to reach you just as much as you are trying to reach them. Your words are building the bridge—plank by plank, nail by nail, word by word.

Imagine the map. You can't see it, but God can. With every word you speak, every dollar you give, every smile that bubbles up in faith, you are closing in toward your goal. You can't see how close you are getting, but God sees it and all of heaven is rooting for you. Can't you hear them? Keep going, Mama! Keep going! It's just around that next bend! You're so close! Just. Keep. Going.

The Hardest Easy

You are doing the only real hard work that is appointed to us as believers. And it's hard, especially for moms. We tend to want to control things in the natural world. But you've stepped into the supernatural, and what worked there does not work here. Jesus said that His yoke was easy. Yes, it's easy. But it's the hardest easy you'll ever go through.

"Let us therefore be zealous *and* exert ourselves *and* strive diligently to enter that rest [of God, to know and experience it for ourselves], that no one may fall *or* perish by the same kind of unbelief *and* disobedience [into which those in the wilderness fell]" (Hebrews 4:11 AMPC).

Understand this. You're not striving and exerting yourself to reach the goal. You're striving and exerting yourself to enter the rest in knowing it's already done. It will challenge you in every way possible. You'll be tempted to doubt. But doubt will only take you back to where you started. Only one thing caused the people in the wilderness to fall—doubt. When they didn't see an immediate solution, they started muttering against God:

"... The whole congregation said ...Why does the Lord bring us to this land to fall by the sword? ... Is it not better for us to return to Egypt?" (Numbers 14:2-3 AMPC).

Did you catch the key word in there? They SAID. They let their doubt become word and the word became flesh. The same process works for us or against us. God did not lead them out of Egypt to destroy them. He led them out to bring them into the Promised Land. They did not see how this would happen, so immediately they turned from the supernatural back to the natural. They were more willing to return to slavery and their old ways of doing things, than to go forward into the promise of abundance.

Just because you can't see your Promised Land yet, doesn't mean you're not walking into it. Keep speaking. Keep believing. Get excited about it, and don't stop. You've gone too far to turn back now.

The House That God Built

For 15 years, we lived in a lovely home—modest, but lovely in its own way. It was set at the end of a cul-de-sac, a small three-bedroom, two-bath 1,800-square-foot Cape Cod that somehow held a family of ten within its walls. Although I loved that home, I frequently looked for a different home that would give us a little more room. I searched real estate sites, picked up magazines at the grocery store, and even collected house plans. All the time, dreaming of something bigger and better. I was grateful for my home but dreamed of more.

Please know that dreaming of bigger and better isn't a sign of discontent. We are made in God's image. God is expansive and abundant. That is why we always have a hunger for more. It's just His nature living through us.

"If I go a day without speaking my proclamations, I feel my day has been incomplete somehow. Interweaving God's word into my daily affirmations is like sending a powerful, supercharged 'rocket' into the heavenly realm."

—Gay-Lea C.

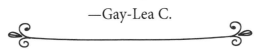

The last year we lived there, I decided to try this whole Hear It/Speak It Formula. I recorded my goals, including this one:

"I live in a spacious home on the water, filled with beautiful treasures and surrounded by beautiful land."

Every day, I played the recording and said it out loud as I walked my neighborhood. I imagined the home. It was white. We could sit outside on the screened porch and see the water. It was one of the big, fancy homes that I would see in those upscale neighborhoods.

I had even picked out the neighborhood. Sometimes, when I was in that area, I would drive through the subdivision, pretending I lived there, saying out loud, "Thank You, God, for my spacious home on the water! I sure do enjoy living in this neighborhood!" When I drove down the street that fed into this neighborhood, I imagined myself pulling in, going home after being out on errands. To the onlooker, I probably appeared to be out of my ever-lovin' mind. But in the spiritual realm, things were happening.

One day I was listening to a podcast by Grant Cardone, advising business owners to rent a home in order to continue investing their dollars into their business and not tie up capital in a liability. Renting? I had never even considered that option, but it made a lot of financial sense—for me and my business. After hearing his advice, I looked online and up popped a home that was listed for rent that very day!

I didn't even think twice. I called the realtor and agreed to meet her the next day to look at the home. I followed the address on my phone and it took me to the exact same neighborhood I had imagined living in. I went down a street, to a cul-de-sac, and there was the home. It was a white home, sitting over the water, with the best view of the lake in the entire neighborhood. It was huge—almost four times the size of the house we were currently living in. It had a pool, a pool house, a playground, Jacuzzi, outdoor kitchen—the works. It even had a guest house on the property. And to top it all off, it was remarkably in our price range. In one day, God moved us into the house. But the pathway to get there had been laid over the past ten months in the supernatural realm, word by word, as I walked and spoke, and walked and spoke.

As I'm finishing up this chapter, I just stepped out of my office to write the rest from the back porch. From here, I have a full view of the lake and can hear the kids playing outside near the playground. A heron just took off over the water and the sun has lit up the sky with pinks and purples as it descends over the trees. There goes God again, showing off.

God wants to show up and show off in your life. He wants to do what you can't. All you have to do is what you can. Don't waste time trying to figure out how He will do it, just trust that He is at work and start speaking up. It's right there. The miracle is in your mouth. Speak it. Keep speaking it. And when you don't see anything happening, speak it again and again. Things are happening. Big things. God said so; and He is a Man of His Word.

STEP FIVE: MAP

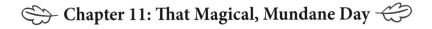 Chapter 11: That Magical, Mundane Day

Being a homeschool mom allows you the freedom to plan your own family schedule. It also does something to your brain that makes you think that you can pretty much take on the entire world and come out without a scratch. My friend Angela makes it look easy. She is a professional photographer, excellent teacher, and business owner, and she loves the Lord. But she's not so good at judging the size and complexity of tasks. She jumps in and learns to swim while she's floundering around and gasping for air. We can all learn a lot from her!

The task she decided to take on would make most of us crumble at the mere thought. Her husband had long weeks of travel, so Angela decided to pack up the five kids, rent an RV, and travel the United States for a month. Yeah. Sure. Why not?

She called me and wanted to make a stop in Virginia so her kids could check out all the rich American history here. But she didn't know where to park her…house. We decided to meet at a grocery store parking lot. I was there early, excited to see my friend. Only a few minutes later, I saw the enormous white RV pulling in to the parking lot. I jumped out of the car and began waving to her and jumping up and down. I started laughing hysterically when I saw this woman, all of 5'2", in the driver's seat of the abominable snow monster on wheels. The thing was a behemoth!

When she parked and stepped out, I noticed she looked like she needed sleep, caffeine, or a good scrubbing. Maybe all three. I gave her a hug and said, "You okay?"

"Do I look okay?" she asked. "I almost got arrested last night and it was 3 a.m. before we found a place to stop."

Her Wi-Fi went out a little before midnight, and she couldn't get any directions into Virginia. She took weird twists and turns and somehow ended up in the worst section of town imaginable. There she was in the abominable snow monster, trying to navigate on tiny roads while lights turned on, dogs started barking, and people piled out of their homes and apartments to watch this strange lady driving her house around the streets in the wee hours of the morning.

At one point, she found herself on a small road with no outlet. She realized she only had one choice—turn that beast around and head out. She backed up, moved forward, backed up, moved forward. In the middle of her 27-point turn, she was stuck across the road, completely blocking it, with the front of her RV in a ditch on one side and the back inches away from the front stoop of an apartment building. To this day, she still can't figure out how she got out of that mess. People were outside sharing food, cracking open some beers, and taking videos—in the middle of the night! Some were nice enough to stand around and help her navigate. Others were just cracking up at the sight. Finally, around 2 a.m., she managed to turn the RV around and head out, right as her Wi-Fi came back on.

If you have ever been caught without a map or directions, you know that feeling of panic. You have no idea how you're going to get to your destination. It's terrifying, especially in an RV after midnight in the hood!

But a lot of moms are living without any navigation. I don't want you wasting time and energy going nowhere. And I certainly don't want you to end up on any dead-end roads. In the MAP step, we are creating your plan, your MAP, to get you to your destination. Grab the wheel of your behemoth life and let's move forward!

Abraham's Kicking Butt and Taking Names

In the Bible, we get a glimpse of a different side of Abraham. His nephew, Lot, had been kidnapped. As a mom, you have a "Mama Bear" instinct, which means if people mess with you, you couldn't care less. But if someone messes with someone you love? That person better start running because you will cut them and not think twice. I know, I know. It's not too Christian, but you know what I'm talking about. We're pack animals. We protect our tribes! If you want to get at someone I love, you gotta get through me first!

Abraham was the same way. He had a "Daddy Bear" instinct when it came to his nephew. When he got word that Lot was kidnapped, Abraham's blood pressure shot up!

"When Abram heard that [his nephew] had been captured,

he armed (led forth) the 318 trained servants born in his own house and pursued the enemy as far as Dan. He divided his forces against them by night, he and his servants, and attacked and routed them, and pursued them as far as Hobah which is north of Damascus. And he brought back all the goods and also brought back his kinsman Lot and his possessions, the women also and the people" (Genesis 14:14-16 AMPC).

Can't you just see it? Abraham tells his hundreds of servants, "C'mon, boys, let's go get 'em!" He not only rescues Lot, but also kicks their butts all the way across town and back and brings back everything—that's errrrrything—they stole! Scripture says "all the goods." Word probably spread fast—don't mess with the big guy, or his nephew!

I'm telling you, the enemy has stolen goods from you. He has robbed you of energy, joy, enthusiasm, and the rightful harvest that belongs to you as a mom. We're creating a plan to get every bit of it back! Abraham had to plan his attack before he could execute it. That's what we're doing—creating a plan so we can attack the day head-on.

Square by Square, Day by Day

I like to consider myself crafty, but I really stink at it. I'd much rather go to Target and buy the wreath than burn 12 layers of skin off my fingers with a hot glue gun. That's why when I decided to make my daughters a quilt, I can only blame it on a momentary lapse of brain function. I realized about two days into the project that I was way out of my league, especially for someone who didn't know how to sew! But I was determined to make the blasted thing. So, each week, I set a goal of one square. That's it. Just one completed square.

In a few months, I finished the quilt. From about 35 feet away, the thing looks great, especially if you're near-sighted. It's not perfect, but it's good enough, it's done, and it keeps them warm at night. The quilt serves its purpose.

"Before learning how to plan my day, I was constantly spinning my wheels. I hustled all day long between laundry, homeschooling, making meals, do this, do that. At the end of the day I was exhausted, and nothing felt finished. My life changed with my MAP. Suddenly, I felt caught up. My family could get out the door on time, and I had time to read a book without guilt. It has truly taken the struggle out of my day to day living!"

—Lacey R.

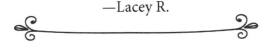

You have a huge purpose for your life. God created you to do miracles and achieve greatness! You don't have to know how to do it all right now. You don't need to figure out the end result. You don't even need to wonder how you're going to get out of debt, or get that weight off, or break out of this slump, or overcome depression. Don't worry about the whole quilt. We're doing one square at a time, and we're doing it together. If that one square turns out okay, the quilt will turn out just fine. We're tackling life square by square, day by day, and creating a beautiful life that will fulfill its purpose. Don't try to figure out your life. Let's just figure out your day. Because if you can master a day, you can master your life.

Jesus understood this principle when He said, "So do not worry or be anxious about tomorrow, for tomorrow will have worries *and* anxieties of its own. Sufficient for each day is its own trouble" (Matthew 6:34 AMPC).

When I was a little kid, my parents gave me a T-shirt that said, "Here comes trouble." I didn't understand what it meant. I thought they were literally changing my name to "Trouble." In retrospect, it would have been a good fit.

I know you, Mama. You made it to Step 5. Play time is over. You ain't checking it out. You're in it to win it. Now here comes trouble! But that's cool. You're ready for it. When life throws trouble at you, you just roll up your sleeves and say, "Bring it!"

Jesus said that worry and anxiety are products of the future, and the future hasn't even happened yet. Why create something that can torment you? That's what we do when we worry. Worrying is like praying for something you don't want to happen. You have the power to create, and when you put energy into negative circumstances or imaginary outcomes, it facilitates that very thing you are trying desperately to avoid.

Jesus said, in effect, "Chill, Girl. I got this." Worry and anxiety are tools of the enemy to get you into tomorrow and off the track of today. All your success happens in the present. It's what you put in today that determines your tomorrow. Jesus also said that each day would have enough trouble of its own. In other words, you don't need to add to it. Just handle today. That's it. But you're not handling it alone.

"...In the world you have tribulation *and* trials *and* distress *and* frustration; but be of good cheer [take courage; be confident, certain, undaunted]! For I have overcome the world. [I have deprived it of power to harm you and have conquered it for you.]" (John 16:33 AMPC).

Sure, we'll have trouble in our days. But the good news is that Jesus has already overcome our days for us. We can get excited and go into each day with confidence because of what Jesus has done. As you create your MAP, know that Jesus has already put His stamp of approval on it. So, let's carpe that diem, Mama!

Making Your MAP

The MAP is not only your guidebook to create a rockin' life, it's also an acronym. It stands for Mundane Action Plan. It's mundane because it seems routine and uneventful. I mean, really, how sexy can making up the bed be? How glamorous is prepping dinner or grocery shopping? It's mundane; but hidden in the mundane is magic. Lisa, one of the moms who went through the Mom Mastery Method, emailed me and said, "OMG! The MAP should stand for Magic Action Plan because it has magically transformed my day!" Okay, I'll go along with that.

#1: Write your real day.

For one day, from the time you get out of bed until you tuck your sweet self back in, write down how you spend your time. You don't have to get super specific with it, just a rough framework will do. For example, when you wake up, do housework, scroll through your phone, work on a business, play with the kids, watch TV, run errands, that sort of thing.

#2: Play detective.

The next day, using that framework as a guide, spend some time with paper and pencil, and do some detective work. Everyone has 24 hours in a day. Some people accomplish amazing amounts, while others spin their wheels. So, channel your inner Sherlock and let's investigate where the time is going. You can use these questions as a springboard:

What activities can I consolidate?
When and how can I invest in myself?
How can I structure this activity better?
What was a good use of my time?
What was a bad use of my time?
What did I do that made me feel energized?
What did I do that made me feel depleted?

What can I delegate?

What can I eliminate?

#*3*: **Write your dream day.**

You've taken a trip before, I'm sure. You've probably planned a vacation and written down everything to pack so you wouldn't overlook anything. That's basically what we're doing in this step. You're creating your "list" that will eventually become your day. Imagine your perfect day: What would it include? Here are a few ideas to get you started.

Wake up early (set the time)

Exercise/meditate

Speak your affirmations

Play with the kids

Do housework/declutter

Make healthy meals

Build my business

Be specific when you design your day. What time would you wake up? What kind of exercise would you do, and for how long? What housework would you get done, and on what days? If you're building a business, what would that look like? Making calls? Setting up email funnels? Following up with clients? Remember, this is your dream day. Dream big, but dream with precision.

"My life needed a complete overhaul! I took the leap of faith, and since applying the Mom Mastery Method, I am off all medication for rheumatoid arthritis for the first time in 19 years! My husband shared with me that he has noticed how much more I'm enjoying motherhood. And probably the most amazing part of my journey is that I am dreaming big dreams for my life for the first time ever!"

—Kim L.

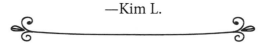

#4: Create your MAP.

We're going to marry those two lists together—the real one and the dream one—and create a happy medium. This will be your MAP. What can you possibly do in 16 hours (you need to sleep, too)? Joellen, one of the awesome women inside Mom Mastery University, did this exercise and found out that she was cleaning the kitchen after dinner, when she had three perfectly healthy teenagers at home. She realized it was time to delegate. When she put them in charge of cleaning up after dinner (and actually executed it), she was able to free up an additional hour each day to get her blog started. This is also a good time to rope in an objective friend who can help you realistically plan your MAP.

Here's what my MAP looks like:

5:30	wake up, devotion
6:00	30 minutes of exercise (usually yoga)

6:30	meditate
6:45	go walking
7:30	shower
8:00	wake up kids and get them started with chores
9:00	homeschooling
11:00	kids (individual studies), me (business)
12:00	lunch break
1:00	read aloud to kids
1:30	kids (reading time), me (business)
2:30	I keep working. If kids are done with school, they have free time.
5:00	prep dinner
6:00	dinner and clean up
7:00	hang out with the family (if a deadline is approaching, work)

WARNING! Please don't look at this and think, 'Wow! Hannah's got her junk together!' This is my MAP; it's much more of a structure than a schedule. Remember, we are all MVPs. We have multiple variables coming at us at all times. Many of us work outside the home, or have special needs kids, or have other obligations that pull at us. We all have our own weirdness that knocks our schedules off track—a kid tells us at the last minute they need foam board for a science project or a leak in the toilet that floods out the bathroom. Don't think for a minute that because you can't stick to a schedule, you can't be structured. We wipe ourselves off and get back up. Sure, you get thrown off your MAP. It's not like it "might" happen. It will happen! You're an MVP. That's when you take a deep breath and dive right back in.

You also have the power to let your MAP evolve with you. It won't stay the same because you don't stay the same. Give yourself grace. Let yourself learn. But don't get stuck in a dead end. Create your MAP and put it to use, tweaking it as you go down the path to success.

Your Bookends

We're going to dive into routines in STEP SIX: MOMENTUM. But there are two routines you need to put inside your MAP from the very beginning. They are your daily bookends—your PM Routine and your AM Routine. Without these essential routines in place, your day is going to spill out all over the place, like Jell-O without a mold. These routines are going to be your framework in which you structure the rest of your day.

Your PM Routine sets the stage. Every great day begins the night before. This is the routine you will do before you go to bed each night to ensure the next day operates as smoothly as possible. My youngest girls do a lot of acting and I can tell you as a backstage mom, that a properly set stage can make or break a performance. Your PM Routine will consist of the following:

- Lay out your outfit for the next day, even accessories.
- If leaving the home, put everything you need by the door.
- Look over tomorrow's schedule and set alarms in your phone if needed.
- Make sure the kids are ready—clothes, lunches, schoolwork.
- Check your meal plan and ingredients for the next day.

- Spend 10 minutes picking up main living areas.

This entire routine shouldn't take longer than 45 minutes. And it will be the best 45 minutes you will invest the entire day. If you think you don't have time for your PM Routine, think about how much time you spend trying on different outfits in the morning, hunting lost keys, searching for homework, and throwing last-minute meals together. This solves all that, so make sure you include it in your MAP. At the outset, give yourself one hour before bed to accomplish it, and you'll be able to shorten that time as you get the hang of it. Plus, you'll sleep so much sweeter when you know you've prepped for the next day.

"My MAP makes even the biggest goals attainable. It works like magic! To think that a small routine, done daily, will compound into the actualization of your goal! Learning this was life changing for me. Thanks, Hannah!"

—Andrea K.

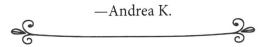

Your AM Routine sets the tone. Have you ever woken up putting out fires? You get out of bed feeling rushed and for the next few hours—or sometimes the rest of the day—you just feel like you're floating along, wading through all the gunk of the day. Well, no more, warrior woman! Those days are over. Instead of letting the day wake you up, turn the tables and wake up the day! Your AM Routine is the routine you will do immediately upon waking up in the morning. It helps you set the tone for the entire day. As goes the first hour of the day, goes the entire day. You know that's true. It's hard to recover from a tough morning, especially for moms. Instead of trying to recover, you'll start out on top! Your AM Routine will consist of the following:

Wake up at least 1-2 hours before anyone else in the house.
Make up the bed (when everyone's out!)
Spend time with God—reading the Bible, devotion, prayer.
Exercise! Even if it's only 15 minutes of stretching—do it!
Shower and get dressed—head to toe, hair and face included.
Eat a healthy breakfast or have a smoothie.

The AM Routine is for you—to make you the most powerful, productive mom you can be! You don't want to hit the ground running. You want to hit it calm, cool, and collected. That's what your AM Routine does for you. You're fueled up, inside and out, head to toe, ready to take on anything life has to throws at you. And, trust me, life loves to throw stuff! They say, "All's well that ends well." But for a mom, it's "All's well that starts well."

If you get a decent night's sleep, then you may notice that in the morning, your energy is higher, your brain is more focused, and you can solve problems better. It's always those decisions we make late at night that prove to be not-so-smart. *Nachos at midnight? Why not!*

Take advantage of this highly productive time by waking up to an alarm (no, a crying baby doesn't count) and doing your AM Routine.

The most successful and profitable people in the world all have one thing in common—they get up early and have a plan. A mom can't necessarily plan her days because they operate so spontaneously. But she can plan her mornings. Seize that time! If you can't carpe the diem, just carpe the morning, and watch your energy, productivity, and mood all elevate!

Your mornings are magical, but you've got to set that time and guard it like Fort Knox guards its gold. There's gold in them thar hills; and there's gold in your morning if you would just get to diggin'. First, you need to set your own time. I need two hours. It's critical for me in order to do everything I want to do.

Tom Ziglar shares one thing he does every morning that has completely transformed his success and productivity. He calls it "the two chairs." He sets two chairs, face-to-face. Each morning, he sits in one chair and imagines Jesus sitting in the other one. He then says these three sentences:

You know my situation.
You're big enough to handle it.
What's your plan?

He shares that this one activity has given him more insight and direction than any other activity he has ever participated in. If you really want to massively improve how you spend your time, then don't waste it on things that aren't going to amount to anything. Get insight from God first thing in the morning and He'll make the rest of the day count.

I know a lot of moms will fight an AM Routine. I did, too. I was convinced I didn't have enough time for that "magical morning" experience and would just start the day running. Then I realized that I had a choice. I could either have 22 hours blessed, or 24 hours cursed. It was a no-brainer. Now I invest those first couple of hours in myself, and the very first thing I do is spend time getting my directions from God. He knows what you don't, so trust Him, and roll those cute buns out of bed!

Can Mom Come Out and Play?

This seems like a lot of work at first. Get up early? Morning and evening routines? But faith without works is dead. Your actions reveal the extent to which you believe something. If you know it's going to rain, you bring along an umbrella. If you know people are showing up for dinner, you make plenty of food. If you believe that God is going to fulfill His promises to you, your behavior shows it, every minute of the day.

"I love my MAP! It's like my brain on paper! It frees my mind of all the constant flowing thoughts and I am able to accomplish more. Also, no more endless to-do lists and scraps of

paper all over the house that I could never find."

—Jessica B.

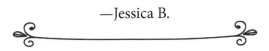

Your life is changing. You already feel things shifting and moving into place. Now is when your faith shows up in your lifestyle. When you treat being a mom like a legitimate career and show up ready to rock it, things change in your favor. You'll have energy you didn't have before. You'll wake up excited. You'll go to bed with that "good" tired feeling of a day well lived. Start working the field, and the harvest will show up. It's a guarantee.

And something even more magical happens. You learn to play again. For too long, you felt you had to earn joy; and because of your workload, you never gave yourself permission. When you create a MAP and follow it, you get to take lovely detours. Your work is work, so your play can be play. The kids get your attention and you're not distracted by the next thing on your list. Joy is your birthright. And your MAP makes that happen.

You Can Do Anything for 24 Hours

I remember when I was a brand-new mom. I was overwhelmed with the task of raising a newborn. And when I blithely volunteered to babysit my friend's newborn for the day, I realized I was in over my head. But I couldn't back out. I had already committed. I could barely take care of one newborn. How was I going to take care of two?

I called my oldest sister in a panic. "Regina, I don't know what to do! I said I would babysit a newborn, and taking care of Kelsey is already overwhelming me!"

She told me what I'm telling you right now—"You can do anything for 24 hours!"

I took a deep breath, hung up the phone, and painted war paint on my face. I didn't need someone to rescue me. I just needed to change my perspective. Heck, yeah, I can do this.

People have done amazing things in 24 hours—

Nabi Salehi of London did 526 haircuts in 24 hours.
Yiannis Kouros of Greece ran 188 miles in 24 hours.
Helge Toft of Norway performed 65 concerts in 24 hours.
Eva Clarke of Australia did 3,737 pull-ups in 24 hours.
"Murs" a music artist in Los Angeles rapped for 24 hours.

You can certainly rock your life for 24 hours! And here's the crazy thing. All you have to do is today. You don't have to worry about all that other stuff. Pretend that this day is it. It's all you have. Put everything into it and run it like you mean business. All you have is right now. Master today, and you will master your life!

Chapter 12: Every Mama
Was Kung Fu Fighting!

It stinks to play a game when you have no skill.

My mom made me try out for the basketball team when I was in high school. I guess she figured since I was nearly as tall as a Lebron James, I must be able to play like him. Seems she forgot about the whole "hand-eye coordination" factor. Since there were all of 113 people in my high school, trying out for the team meant you were in it, no matter how badly you played the sport.

I remember sitting on the bench, praying that the score would stay close so the coach wouldn't put me in. If we ever started to climb up on the scoreboard, I would panic. "Please, Lord, I will go to Africa and wash feet all day long. Just please don't let the coach put me in the game."

The most successful scenario would be for me to dress in my costume for the game (I didn't know they were called uniforms until halfway through the season), and get through the game without touching a basketball.

Sometimes, success evaded me. Our team would blow the other team out of the water. I would get more nauseous with each point until that dreaded moment would happen. The coach would look down the bench and see me sitting at the very end of the row, trying to avoid eye contact and magically morph into the bleachers. He would call my name. I would pretend I didn't notice and start studying my cuticles. He would call my name again, more loudly. Eventually, I would have to drag myself out to the court.

I did score that first season. But it was in the other team's basket. True story.

I didn't have any basketball skills, so I hated the game.

That summer, I went to camp and spent every single day of that intense week learning how to play the game (my mom made me). The rest of the summer, I practiced for hours every single day.

That fall, I came back and became starting center on the high school team. My highest score in a game was 29 points. And, yes, every single one went in our team's basket. I went from hating the game to loving the game.

You don't have any choice. You're playing the time game whether you realize it or not. You can either stay clueless and frustrated, wondering why you get nothing accomplished and feel exhausted every day. Or you can master the skills and kick some serious butt.

If you're going to overcome Mom Fatigue Syndrome, you can't just learn time management skills. That's for other folks. You need to learn supreme-level skills. You need to take time management to an art form. You need to become a Time Ninja!

So, come on, Grasshopper. Let's do some Kung Fu Fighting and warp time like The Last Airbender bends ... air.

Different Lives, Different Rules

Time management is different for moms. We don't play the same games other people play, so we can't go by the same rules.

I remember listening to a podcast by a successful motivational coach. The topic was time management, and I thought, 'This guy's a pro. I'm going to get some good material here.'

One of his tips? Give one task 100 percent undivided attention for a straight 50 minutes. Then for 10 minutes, find a spot away from your work, preferably with a view of nature. Sit cross-legged in that spot and meditate for ten minutes, repeating the mantra, "I am now emptying my mind. I am refreshed and renewed and ready to fully engage in my next project."

I turned off the podcast.

This may work for Mr. Motivation Man, but it doesn't work for Mama. Solutions for SCPs are usually headaches for MVPs.

First of all, even if you had three padlocks on the door, 50 minutes of uninterrupted time is impossible for moms. Even if we could do it, I'm pretty sure in that time, a kid would get electrocuted, or the dirty laundry would stage a coup and take over the house. And meditate? Let me see here. First let me look at nature and find a focal point. Should it be that half-naked Barbie in the middle of the lawn? Or maybe the dead flowers in the pots by the back door? And a mantra? Hmm, how about, "Don't touch me for ten minutes and I'll give you candy."

Let's get real. We're a different breed; we need different skills.

Time Ninja Skill #1: Know Your Enemy

A true ninja studies her opponent. She doesn't just jump into a fight and expect to win. She first gets to know who she's fighting. When it comes to fighting for your time, you've got a very real enemy.

John 10:10 tells us that "the enemy comes to steal, kill, and destroy." And Satan is after your time. Time is your #1 resource, not money. You can always make more money. You can't make more time.

But why does he want your time? It's not like he can use it for anything. That sucker is already defeated. The reason he wants your time is the same reason he wants your money, your relationships, and anything else that belongs to you. He wants it because he knows it's the easiest way to get your peace. And if he has your peace, he has you right where he wants you.

"Until learning how to manage my time, I had constant to-do

list overwhelm. I'd write everything down and then not know where to start, so nothing would get done. I'm getting so much more done, and I am so much more peaceful!"

—Erica C.

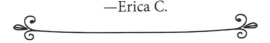

He loves to throw you off your game and make you feel overwhelmed. He'll guilt you into taking on too much and then throw condemnation in your face and tell you what a loser you are when you can't do everything. He'll try to convince you that your tasks will be harder and more time-consuming than they are, just to keep you from tackling them. He'll toss distractions at you from every direction to get you to lose your focus and screw up your priorities.

Know your enemy, Mama. He's crafty, but he's stupid; and he can't come up with any new tricks. Don't fall for them. Ninjas don't do that sort of thing.

Time Ninja Skill #2: Number Your Days (and Minutes)

One of my greatest ninja weapons is my egg timer. That little ticker is more valuable than nunchucks and ninja stars combined. Its power is in that little sound it makes; "tick, tick, tick." When I have a task to do, I set the timer, and that little tick keeps me focused on the task at hand. Why? Because it's numbering my minutes.

Psalm 90:12 reminds us how important it is to keep track of time.

"So teach us to number our days, that we may get us a heart of wisdom" (AMPC).

Check it out. It says, "teach us." That means time management does not come naturally. It's a learned skill. And since we're doing ninja training here, we're going to take that "number our days" thing a bit further. We're going to number our minutes! It's easy to forget that our years are made of months, months are made of days, and days are made of minutes. We tend to think we have all the time in the world, but we have exactly 1440 minutes a day.

Train yourself to stop thinking in hours and half-hours. You're not a day planner or a phone app. You're a human being who has a beautifully spontaneous and fluid life. Learn to think right NOW. When the need strikes, strike the need. Don't wait until that minute hand hits a designated mark. Do it now!

When we understand the finite nature of time, we can plug into an infinite source of power to manage it. God wants to work through you to do amazing things, but it's going to require your participation. And that clock is tickin'! We tend to expand or contract time depending upon our experience with the task. For example, a day at the beach flies by for me because I absolutely love it. It's one of my favorite places in the world. When my husband is at the beach, it seems to last forever. He hates it. The sun, the sweat, the sand in his shoes (yes, he wears shoes at the beach)—it's all torture to him. A day at the beach feels like it lasts 20 minutes to me. For my husband? Forty hours!

I'm challenging you to do something for me: Time yourself! I bet you'll be shocked at how many minutes it takes to do some of your dreaded tasks. I did this and was shocked that it only takes me 7 minutes to fold a load of laundry, 5 minutes to clean a bathroom, and 3 minutes to mop the kitchen. (I said I do it; I never said I do it perfectly!)

Time Ninja Skill #3: Beware the Time Bandits

They're everywhere. They're lurking on your phone and computer; they're hiding in the television and calling you up for favors. They're even knocking on your door with opportunities. Let me just break it down for you: If they're not for you, they're against you! Moms are especially targeted when it comes to time bandits. And that's exactly why we need to be especially on our guard to protect ourselves.

First, we gotta tackle the screens: Facebook, Instagram, Hulu, Netflix, Snapchat, and whatever else emits a tempting warm glow onto your face. I like to compare these to water skiing. If you've ever been water skiing, you know there is an art to it. It's so much fun to speed along, holding on tight, skimming across the surface of the water. But then you get comfortable and you start hot doggin' it. You're like, "Oh, I got this. Watch me work it!"

You let go with one hand. Then you start weaving back and forth. Then you try lifting up one leg. Before you know it, you're flipping over your skis, thigh-slapping the water, and getting a mouthful of lake.

Lesson? Don't get comfortable with screens. They'll drown you. Be aware of the amount of time you spend staring at a screen. Our society is in danger of using phones as default mechanisms. Whenever life pauses, we immediately reach for a phone to fill empty space. This poses a huge problem because empty space is where we do all our creative thinking and problem-solving. Moms must continually think creatively and solve problems. It comes with the job. But if we don't allow that space in our lives, we don't have that opportunity. We get stressed out, but don't leave ourselves any emptiness to process the stressors and come up with solutions. You need a little "empty" in your life. Start becoming aware of the "phone default mode," and put that little bugger away.

"I feel WAY more peace! When I see something that needs to be done while I'm busy with something else, I know it has a place and will get done. That has removed a LOT of stress!"
—Francina G.

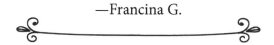

Anyway, you can't complain about the piles of dirty laundry when it takes less than 5 minutes to sort and wash a load, and you've already spent over 18 minutes on Instagram. Yep, I just went there.

But time bandits aren't just electronic. They are living, breathing human beings, too. They are the people who want to talk for hours on end about nothing or get you to do them a favor. Be wary of these bandits. They'll steal your time and leave you bankrupt. As a wise person once told me, people who have nothing to do will often want to do it with you.

You have a lot to do, Mama. You're shaping generations. You're building a future. You're changing this world. Value your contributions and kick the bandits to the curb. With love, of course.

Time Ninja Skill #4: Focus on One Thing at a Time

Do you remember that scene in *Finding Nemo* when Dory and Marlin (Nemo's dad) drop onto a boardwalk that is covered with seagulls. All of a sudden, the birds all start squawking, "Mine! Mine! Mine!" as they stare hungrily at the fish.

It's a perfect picture of a mom's life. She is surrounded by tasks that are all screaming at her simultaneously—"Mom! Mom! Mom!" The question is not, IF she is going to put out a fire that day, the question is which one?

Moms must be multitaskers. At first, singular focus seems counter-intuitive. However, don't confuse multitasking with multi-focusing. Your brain can only focus on one thing at a time. If people say they can focus on more than one thing simultaneously, that just means they just have learned to switch back and forth rapidly.

So, what's wrong with that?

A lot. Our brains are muscles, and just like any muscle, it can get fatigued. Decision-making burns the most glucose of any other activity in your brain. And when you burn glucose, you get fatigued. Ever wonder why your brain starts getting foggy as the day goes on? It's because you're a mom, and you have trained yourself to switch back and forth from multiple stimuli that keep squawking at you, "Mine! Mine! Mine!"

You can multitask with the best of them, but you've got to learn how to singularly focus if you want to overcome that fatigue and fogginess.

"The MAP is a tool that makes a total difference. It's a plan to get where I want to be! When I forget to use it, I feel unproductive and like I've wasted a day. It tells me where I'm headed and how to get there!

—Bridgette S.

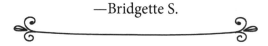

God gave us a perfect example of singular focus when He created the world. Day One, He focused on light. That's it. He was singularly focused in that direction, which is why it turned out so great and only took Him a day! When He created the water, He wasn't worried about the animals He was going to stick in it. He was present at that moment, solely focused on that day's purpose.

We can radically improve our performance and save ridiculous amounts of time when we learn to focus on one thing at a time. Sure, you can multiTASK, but you can only wrap your brain around one thing at a time.

For example, you can do a physical activity and a mental one simultaneously. You can do the elliptical while you watch a sermon. You can fold laundry while you tell the kids a story. You can clean the kitchen while you listen to a podcast. This is because the physical activity is done on automatic. You don't have to make any decisions while you do that. In fact, I'm pretty sure I've cleaned the kitchen in my sleep before.

But mental focus can only go in one direction at a time. I can't even communicate how vitally important your task is as a mom. Don't waste this precious time. Be present now. When those thoughts start jumping all over the place, pull them in, take authority, and be here now.

Time Ninja Skill #5: Tie a Bow Around It

I love Christmas, and I love shopping, which conveniently go well together. And one of my favorite parts of Christmas shopping is bringing home the packages, wrapping them up, and tying beautiful bows around them. I've never understood why my kids love those "peel and stick" pre-made bows. I would much rather pick out a beautiful coordinating ribbon, tie a pretty bow, and curl the ribbon on a pair of scissors.

And that's just what you've got to do as a mom, every day of your life. You've got to foster a habit of completion and tie a bow around it!

Moms must be highly distracted in order to care for our children. It's just how God made us. Survival, Mama! But because of this distractible nature, we often only do about 85 percent of our tasks. We fold our laundry, but never put it away. We wash the dishes, but leave the counters messy. We take care of the mail that comes in the house, except for those few letters and bills that we don't know what to do with. I get it. That last 15 percent is usually the hardest part. We grow tired of the current task, and emotionally we feel like we "did our time" by attending to most of it. We often work on tasks just enough to get us out of the pain of being bothered by it, but not quite into the joy of completing it. We wrap the package, but forget about the last 15 percent—the bow!

It takes a lot less time to do something right than it does to do something over. If you finish the task completely and tie a bow around it, it doesn't have a chance to fall apart, get lost, or stack up. Plus, you feel like the mega-accomplished amazing superhero that you are.

Fight the urge, Mama. Do that last 15 percent. Just today, that's all. Tie a bow around everything and watch the difference it makes in your life, your energy, and your outlook. Tomorrow, you can make that decision again. But, remember, Grasshopper, you are singularly focused on today. See how the ninja training builds on itself?

Time Ninja Skill # 6: Calendarize Your Life

When I mastered this skill, the clouds parted, the sun shone down, and a chorus of angels began singing, "Walking on Sunshine" by Katrina and the Waves. I'm pretty sure you will have the same experience.

First, say goodbye to your to-do list! A to-do list is a HUGE time-waster. It's basically a homeless shelter for tasks. You have a lot to do, and every task needs a designated home in your life. Instead of just lumping them all together on one piece of paper, you've got to become more strategic about this.

"Learning how to manage my time has increased productivity through the roof! I've cut transitions way down because I don't have to figure out what to do next. I know what's coming and there's no stress about it."

—Sheryl P.

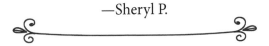

All moms must deal with clutter. And a cluttered day operates by the same principle. It's just a bunch of junk tossed together and it causes stress and anxiety, which you do NOT need in your life! So, we're going to declutter your "to do" list. You tackle it the same way you tackle a cluttered closet or kitchen cabinet. You pull all that junk out, and decide about each little piece, taking one of three actions:

Give it away.

Throw it away.

Put it away.

So, grab that to-do list and look at every little task on there:

Give it away: This may come as a newsflash, but you don't have to do everything. Sometimes pride makes us overload our schedules because we have a primal need to feel needed and important. Let go of that. Can you delegate it? Can you get your family members involved or pay someone to take over this task? You're already doing the most important work. You don't have to add to it.

Throw it away: You know there are things on your to-do list that have camped out there for several weeks. Why not just do something crazy and bold and scratch those suckers off? Maybe it's just not a good time to paint the living room or get that picture framed. Give yourself permission to not do some stuff and experience how good that feels.

Put it away. This is where your calendar comes into play. Instead of adding a task to a to-do list, you will immediately go to your calendar and give it a home. No more homeless shelter! Give it a slot in a day and stick to it! This not only gives you an awesome plan of attack, but it alleviates all the stress that comes with looking at that overwhelming to-do list.

Time Ninja Skill #7: Build Your Wall

In the Bible, Nehemiah dedicated himself to rebuilding the walls of Jerusalem. No small task, but he knew he served a mighty big God. If anyone can teach us about how to manage our resources as moms, it's this guy. And one thing he had going for him was his keen ability to say "No" to distractions.

When Nehemiah's enemies saw what he was attempting to do, they laughed at him. They figured the task was impossible. But when he started making headway, they muffled their laughs and raised their eyebrows. When his actions began leading to real progress, they knew they had to do something to throw him off his game, so they went for one of the most reliable weapons of the enemy—distraction.

"Now when Sanballat, Tobiah, Geshem the Arab, and the rest of our enemies heard that I had built the wall and that there was no breach left in it, although at that time I had not set up the doors in the gates, Sanballat and Geshem sent to me, saying, Come, let us meet together in one of the villages in the plain of Ono. But they intended to do me harm. And I sent messengers to them, saying, I am doing a great work and cannot come down. Why should the work stop while I leave to come down to you? They sent to me four times this way, and I answered them as before" (Nehemiah 6:1-4 AMPC).

Understand this, Mama. Satan does not want you to make progress. You have a huge task to do. It's no small job to raise future generations, build a peaceful home, and establish abundance and prosperity for your family. But you serve a big God who is well able to accomplish this and more through you.

Don't get tempted to go into the valley of "Ono."

"Ono! I just wasted 45 minutes on Facebook
watching stupid videos!"
"Ono! My text chime went off and I got
wrapped up in that conversation."
"Ono! I can't believe I just spent the last hour
watching that talk show."

When those distractions raise their bright, sparkly heads, just channel some Nehemiah. First, realize the intent. They are not there to promote you or bless you. They are there to distract you from what is most important. They intend to do you harm. Wise up, Sugar Pie! Just say "No!" to "Ono!" Just send them the same message that Nehemiah sent to his distractions:

I am doing a great work and cannot come down!

Don't come down, Mama. Don't lower yourself to those distractions beneath you. Stay on target and build your wall. You not only have time on your side, you have the favor of God. Now, go get 'em!

STEP SIX: MOMENTUM

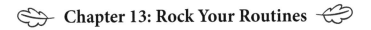 Chapter 13: Rock Your Routines

This is the Momentum step and we're putting routines to work for us. Momentum is the Big Mo! It's what keeps you going even when you want to quit.

When my youngest daughter, Kenna, learned to ride a tricycle, she rode it all over the main floor of the house (yeah, we're that family). She started in the kitchen, biked through the dining room, down the hall, into the living room, then slammed on the brakes and drifted across the sitting room, just before biking through the kitchen and starting the loop all over again. Sometimes, my son would put on *The Fast and the Furious* soundtrack when she started her loop just for effect.

Once that firecracker got started, she just couldn't stop! Around and around she went. Her siblings had to get out of her way or risk getting pummeled. She did this so much that eventually, she completely wore off the finish on the wood floor of the sitting room with her "drift trail."

That's Momentum right there! She was only able to drift across the floor because she had pedaled and pedaled and built up speed. The repetition wore the finish clean off! There it was—tracks of beige, unfinished wood in the middle of the honey-colored pine.

If I had set the goal to strip the finish from the floors, I would have resorted to chemical strippers, sanders, plotted out a weekend to do it, and probably never got to it. When tasks seem difficult, we tend to avoid them. This is why many moms stay stuck in old habits that are feeding into Mom Fatigue Syndrome—not getting enough sleep, eating poorly, not exercising, keeping a messy house, and rushing from task to task. We often overestimate the difficulty of the task and underestimate the ease of routines.

But if routines are so easy, then why don't we do them? The answer, sweet friend, lies right there between your ears.

Beware the Brain!

The mom brain is quite a piece of work. Have you ever wondered why it's so hard to finish what you start, stay motivated, quit bad habits, or break out of a rut? Well, for the most part you are living your life on auto-pilot. You don't wake up and think:

'Should I brush my teeth?'
'Should I put on my pants?'
'Should I check my phone?'

These are all just automatic behaviors. You don't think about them; you just do them. But there was a time, a long time ago, when you actually did have to think about them. You had to decide to brush your teeth when you were just learning how to work that toothbrush, or put on your pants when you didn't want to get caught in your underwear, or check your phone when it was brand new to you.

In a psychological study, researchers found that 95% of human behavior is done unconsciously (auto-pilot), with only 5% of behavior being attributed to conscious choices. What does this mean? This means that, for the most part, we're not even thinking about what we're doing. We're just doing it. Wow. Scary. But even scarier is what it means for moms. We spend most of our time on autopilot! We're surviving, but not necessarily thriving. And when Mama ain't happy, ain't nobody happy.

"Routines saved me! Before the Mom Mastery Method I was just doing what I had to do and grudgingly doing it. I hated every minute, but now that I have my routines my days go so much smoother. If I get nothing else done except my AM and PM routines I am still way ahead of the pack!"

—Lori P.

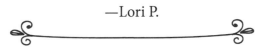

Not only that but making decisions isn't as easy as it looks. Decisions actually burn up a lot of glucose in your brain and after a while, this creates fatigue. Just like a car running out of gas and sputtering to a halt, your brain runs out of glucose and, suddenly, you think it's a great idea to post a video on Facebook of you twerking to Beyoncé. Not a smart idea, I know. But you can't always think clearly when your brain is running on empty.

That's why it sometimes feels like a struggle to change behavior. Behavior is predominantly automatic. We don't always do what we should do; we do what we are accustomed to doing.

The Mom Fog Is Real!

Moms live a unique life. We're MVPs. We don't have the luxury of same-old, same-old; and we rarely live by any set routine because of the constant array of demands placed on us. Our career requires us to make cognitive decisions quickly and frequently. We may load up our brains with fuel in the morning, but by the afternoon, the glucose has burned up and all we have left are automatic responses. And for the sleep-deprived mom, she doesn't even have that morning luxury. Autopilot has taken over. Ever started a diet in the morning and by the afternoon you've eaten an entire row of Oreo cookies? Yep, you can blame your brain, not your stomach.

The Mom Fog just got real!

So, what do you do? Stay stuck in the fog? No way, Mama. The solution lies in taking the decision-making process totally out of it. You can't think your way out of this. You must retrain your brain. When you can take successful behaviors and turn them into automatic responses, you have stumbled upon the secret of routines. You've not only learned how to tame the brain, you've just cleared the fog, too!

John C. Maxwell, author, speaker, and wildly successful entrepreneur, said, "You will never change your life until you change something you do daily. The secret of your success is found in your daily routine."

It's so true! If the cake of the Mom Mastery Method is inside-out growth, then routines make up the icing on top. Moms are creatures of habit because habit doesn't require much thought (something we've depleted by lunchtime). So, what would happen if we took all the thought out if it, and used the power of habit to work for us instead of against us?

That's the power of routines!

Abraham, the Routine Rockstar

If anyone knew the power of routines, it was Abraham. Day and night, night and day, he went about doing what he needed to do. And because of his routines, he became very wealthy in all areas of life.

But Abraham wasn't always skipping through life with his dayplanner tucked under his arm and a smile on his face. He had some disappointments; big disappointments.

At one time in his career, he shared his home with his nephew, Lot, and because of the blessing on his life (and on Lot's life because of the partnership), they had both became too wealthy and expansive to share a home. I know, big problem, right?

They decided to part ways, so Abraham did the honorable thing. He told Lot he could take his pick of the land and Abraham would take the other. Lot looked left and right—on one side it was a lifeless desert. On the other side, green and lush. Lot chose the most promising-looking place, and Abraham was left with the "No Man's Land" (which proves you can't always go by what you see).

As a natural response, Abraham was a bit disappointed, but God showed up.

"The Lord said to Abram after Lot had left him, Lift up now your eyes and look from the place where you are, northward and southward and eastward and westward; For all the land which you see I will give to you and to your posterity forever. And I will make your descendants like the dust of the earth, so that if a man could count the dust of the earth, then could your descendants also be counted. Arise, walk through the land, the length of it and the breadth of it, for I will give it to you" (Genesis 13:14-17 AMPC).

God was basically saying, "Bro, chill. I can take a desert and turn it into Disneyland. Don't be fooled by appearances. I am your source; the land is not. Let's get to it!"

What were Abraham's directions in order to prosper? Get your butt up and start walking. God would give him everything He promised, but Abraham couldn't receive it sitting still. He had to get up and do something about it. God didn't tell him how He was going to prosper him, He just told him to get up out of his pity party and start walking.

"Having a routine completely changed my life! I started to realize I could make progress in every area of my life. I started exercising when I thought I had no time, spending time with God, feeling more prepared for my day and able to handle random circumstances thrown my way!"

—Becky B.

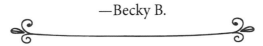

No matter what condition you were in when you arrived here, God is ready to prosper you in bigger and better ways than you can imagine. But you can't get there sitting still. You've got to walk it out, day by day, putting routines into practice that walk you into your promised land. Don't be fooled by what you see. It could look like you are in a desert of no opportunity, missed dreams, and broken promises. Give it to God and let Him do what He does best.

You were born to be blessed. You were designed to live a life of peace, which in Hebrew is "shalom," meaning harmony, wholeness, completeness, prosperity, welfare and tranquility. According to Ephesians 6:15, you've been fitted with the shoes of the gospel of peace. And those boots were made for walking, not kicking back in the easy chair. So, strap 'em on and let's go!

Rung by Rung

Most people tend to see success as luck. Those moms with the clean houses, lots of energy, and having fun with their kids—they must just be lucky. They must have a more supportive spouses, more money, a faster metabolism, or something hidden in their medicine cabinet.

As long as you think it's luck, you will place a wall between you and your success. It's not luck. It's routine. Each day, every day, they do the small steps that lead to the huge success.

I remember when I was at one of the lowest points in my life. The house was a cluttered wreck. We were deep in debt and borrowing from one card to pay another. I was overwhelmed, depressed, and suffered from anxiety. And on top of that, I was out of shape and suffered from horrible allergies. I kept praying for God to help me. Maybe someone would show up at the front door with a check to pay off our debts, or I could find a magic diet that would help me get more energy. Perhaps someone could come in and help me get the house organized, or maybe there was a medication that could take care of my anxiety and allergies.

I can see myself now—stuck in that deep pit of helplessness. I was asking God for help, when He had already tossed down the ladder for me to climb out.

Jesus told the lame man, "Arise, pick up your mat, and walk." He was telling me, just like He told that lame man and just like God told Abraham, "Arise, pick your butt up, and climb." Each rung was a routine that I incorporated in my life. Day by day, rung by rung, my life started to take form. I arose out of that pit and into the light.

"I hardly recognize my life. I was completely hopeless, frustrated, and in a depressed mess before the Mom Mastery Method. Since plugging in I have regained hope as well as found purpose in my life as a mom! I have gained a leel of confidence like I have never had before. I am truly grateful for God bringing me to MMU! We have made a crazy financial goal and have been going above and beyond that goal on a weekly basis. We have also been able to pay $1,522.86 of debt within the first 30 days of plugging in!"

—Sovilla C.

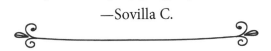

Understand that God wants to help you. He has already done everything He needs to do. He has given you the power and the authority to create the life you desire. He has given you His Word to claim as yours. He has infused you with strength. And He has tossed down the ladder. Take my hand, let's climb out—rung by rung, routine by routine.

The little steps may seem insignificant at first, but the results are staggering. You don't need a major overhaul. You just need to create the right routines. Create the routines, and the routines will create you.

Let's create the best you ever!

The Colossal Myth

You know how it goes—"Faster than a speeding bullet, more powerful than a locomotive, able to leap tall buildings in a single bound..."

That's life in the comics, my friend, and Wonder Woman underwear is about as close as we're going to get to that reality. Sure, you can have superhero abilities, but the reality is more like this:

"Able to leap tall buildings in a series of small, incremental, seemingly insignificant steps taken consistently over a duration of time ..."

I know. It doesn't sound as glamorous or sexy (like those Wonder Woman panties); but what routines lack in sexy, they make up for in success.

There's a myth that is extremely popular right now, and it's the Colossal Myth. It says that we need to reach success in a "single bound." We want the colossal results, and we want them now. We want the washboard abs in 90 days, the six figures in 6 months, the decluttered house in a weekend. But what comes up, must go down. And fast results are often short-lived. You're in it for the long haul, Mama, and you cannot sustain quick fixes over the duration. The answer is not in the hustle. That's the world's way. We want something that will last! Goodness gracious, the last thing moms need is another roller-coaster ride!

"Since joining Mom Mastery University I have so much peace in my life. I am a foster mom and that comes with a lot of stress. I was always second guessing myself. I had no confidence and was living in fear. This is all gone. Thanks to the Mom Mastery Method, I have confidence. I am enjoying time with my children. I have more patience with my special needs daughter. I allow myself to have fun with my kids and it has made a huge difference in our relationship. My house is clean and a place of peace. I love walking through the front door! I am amazed with the positive changes in my life!"

—Courtney S.

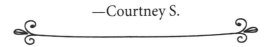

Have you ever seen a huge skyscraper being built? At first, it seems like it's taking forever. All you see are massive machines, traffic cones, and hard hats. There's a lot of noise and commotion. It's messy, dirty, and stinky, and you're thinking, 'Would you just get on with it already?' Then, it seems like overnight, a huge, gleaming skyscraper just emerges from the landscape. Foundations are messy, noisy, even hazardous. But once you get the foundation in place, the building practically takes care of itself. Your life is a lot like that. Beginnings are messy.

As you lay the foundation for your skyscraper life, you will discover that it stinks at times. It's difficult to create motivation when you just want to take a nap on the sofa when you're so accustomed to old ways of thinking. It's difficult to speak positively when everything in you wants to gripe and complain. But you're laying the foundation, and that is the messiest part. Everyone wants overnight success, but it usually leaves behind a failure hangover.

As you develop your routines, understand that you are laying the foundation for your colossal success story. You will emerge from the landscape and people will ask, "How did you do this? How do you have so much energy? How do you have such a positive attitude?" They will want that secret "24-hour" colossal myth. When you tell them your secret: "Small, incremental, seemingly insignificant steps taken consistently over a duration of time," their eyes may just glaze over as they change the subject.

Not everyone wants to do what they have to do to get where they want to go. But you do. I know that because you're still here. You're still plugging away. I also know that for you, success is not just a probability, it's inevitable.

Colossal results happen with consistent effort. It's not the single bounds, but the baby steps that will get you where you want to go. And, until you can be diligent in the dark, you'll never be promoted in the light. God promotes us. He doesn't transport us. God won't do for us what He has given us the power and authority to do for ourselves. And creating routines is something each of us can do. It's easy, but it doesn't always look pretty.

Building the foundation for a skyscraper is never a pretty sight. And, I don't care who you are, 5am never looks good on anyone. There you are, pulling yourself out of bed with hair going in a thousand different directions and smudges of old mascara under your eyes. But there you are, with your Bible and a cup of coffee fueling yourself up for the day. There you sit, with your notebook and your bills, working out your budget There you are, on that treadmill for 20 minutes. You're doing it, Girl! And that's all you need to do—just show up!

"I finally feel confident enough to have someone over for the first time in YEARS! My financial credit rating has moved steadily up about 180 points since May. My husband is happier and says things are the best they have been since we have been married. He said it best when he said, '$65 a month or $65,000, I don't care because it's worth it!' He keeps threatening to write "that Hannah lady" a letter to give her a piece of his mind—because he is so happy!"

—Bonnie D.

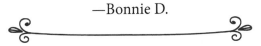

Success is fruit, not fast food. You must grow it over time. If you want to be bored out of your mind, just park yourself by an apple tree and watch an apple grow. Nothing spectacular. It looks the same every single day. That's the deception of routines. You don't realize how powerful they are because nothing seems to change. Every day, you just keep doing those routines, not realizing what is going on behind the scenes. You are training your brain and shaping your will. You wonder if anything is happening, then suddenly, you realize the apple is ripe—

Can I actually fit into those pants?
What? Is that a collarbone peeking out?
How did all that money show up in my savings account?
Huh? Did my child really just obey me the first time?
Did I actually watch that movie and not fall asleep on the sofa?
How in the world did this house get organized?

You're going to shock yourself with the astronomical results that happen when you just keep showing up. Each day, every day.

Routines Are Easy Peasy

I remember when my husband ordered P90X, the intense workout program. I got all motivated, ready to get in shape with him. The first day, I threw up. Not even kidding. I stopped the push-ups just in time to make it to the bathroom and hurl. I've found I work much better with a "yoga, brisk walk, dance to 80s music" kind of fitness program. People often approach the path to success with this colossal myth that it must be hard. If it's not painful, it must not be working.

But according to Matthew 11:30, His yoke is easy and His burden is light!!

Routines are deceptively easy, which is really good and really bad. They're good because they are easy to execute. I mean, honestly, how hard is it to make up a bed? How hard is it to lay out your clothes before you go to bed? Or drink two cups of water? Or dance to a song? They're easy, which is awesome for us. But bad, too, because we subconsciously feel that they're almost too easy. We mistake easy for insignificant, so we tend to skip out on them. Routines are easy, but remarkably powerful. Don't let the ease fool you.

Time's on Your Side

Routines are powerful because you are putting time to work for you. Time is just a tool. It's not partial. You can use it anyway you want. You can use it to build your skyscraper or tear it down. I've heard it said that first, you make your habits, then your habits make you, whether those habits are good or bad. And the hardest habits to create are the best ones to have.

But time can't go to work for you until you start. The best time to start creating good routines? About five years ago. The second best? Right now! Don't ever think it's too late or you're too far gone. Five years from now you will be grateful you started today. All of heaven's armies are standing around, waiting for you to grab that first rung and start pulling so they can get to work helping you out. God's greatest desire is to bless you, but you've got to give Him something to work with. And you've got to do it now!

"My scale says 165 pounds—my goal weight! I'm back in my goal jeans at age 52. I had seriously doubted that would ever happen but God has added His super to my natural and, since joining Mom Mastery University, I've lost 19 pounds and my blood sugar has dropped from 134 to 105!"

—Kelly T.

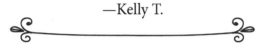

That elephant in the room? Your anxiety? Your fatigue? Your depression? Weight? Clutter? Whatever it is, you've been staring at it for way too long. It's time to eat that sucker! How do you eat an elephant? One bite at a time. I know that elephant looks huge. I know you'd rather just get a bulldozer and shove it out of the way. But the little bites always, always work! It's just so easy, we don't realize how powerful those little bites are. Sure, it takes a while, but that elephant isn't going anywhere so you may as well get to chewing.

Make Some Montage Magic

We've all seen the feel-good movies. The loser becomes the winner in all of 3½ minutes; the street kid who trains in the gym and rises to the top of the fight club; the schoolteacher who transforms a classroom of students; the athlete with the odds stacked against him who becomes an Olympic champion. You know how it goes—the main character gets a sudden dose of inspiration then you cue the music. During the song, you see the montage—the main character showing up, putting in the work, getting better and better, and then … success! The song ends, and our hero is back on top again.

Wouldn't that be awesome if it really worked that way? We could just put on the Rocky theme song, do some fist punches, and we'd be there. Happy Ending. Scene closes. Roll credits. Life is good.

Your success story is not a montage. It takes a lot more time, energy, and freaking hard work than you can pack into any song. But maybe there's more to this whole montage thing than we think. Maybe we can use that same power that pumps us up in the theater to motivate us at home. All montages use the same formula that directors, screenplay writers, and editors use when they're creating a blockbuster. And it works like magic.

Steps to Using the Montage Magic:

Step 1—Find your song. Sometimes a hype song is all a mama needs to get her up and moving with her routines. Remember, it's all baby steps. We establish Momentum by executing those small tasks that make such a huge difference over time. But to get Momentum, sometimes you need a jump start. Pick your "theme song" and blast it when you need to get back in that state of accomplishment.

Step 2—Return to your "why." Check out any success story movie. There's always a quick scene that precedes a montage where the character returns to the reason she started the journey in the first place. If you ever feel like not making the bed, folding the clothes, or making the calls, just go back to that moment that kicked off the journey. It could be pain or pleasure, desperation or inspiration; but there was a moment when your excuse to stop became your reason to keep going. Return to it.

Step 3—Get your script. Every movie has certain key phrases that tug at your heart and seem to wrap up the entire story in one sentence:

You had me at "Hello."
Toto, I've a feeling we're not in Kansas anymore.
You is kind. You is smart. You is important.
Go ahead. Make my day.
May the force be with you.

There are certain key phrases that will make you go for 100 percent when you want to stop at 85 percent. They give you that last little push to keep going. When I want to stop cleaning the kitchen after only a few dishes, or just leave the laundry for another day, I tell myself out loud, "How you do anything is how you do everything." It pushes me to complete a task and perform at the level of excellence that I want to characterize everything I do in life.

"I am so blessed! I am not the same woman I was before join-

ing Mom Mastery University. I keep saying Hannah Keeley is changing my life. And my husband has said the same. THANK YOU, Hannah! Thank you for MMU!"

—Anna P.

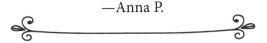

Your script will also help you get back on track when you start running off the rails. Much of your script can be found in those affirmations you speak daily. For example, I am often tempted to snack on unhealthy food or to overeat. When this happens, I quickly recall one of my affirmations, which is "I eat for energy and stop when I've had enough." Those words are enough to make me put away the potato chips. So, what's your script? Find it and speak it! And don't let any of those old limiting or disparaging dialogues find their way into your new screenplay.

Step 4—Collect the clips. Every montage is full of short video clips that reveal the journey. Go ahead and put yourself into the end scene, where you've met your goals. This affirms your new identity. In your mind, see the little clips that will take you there—jumping out of bed when the alarm goes off, setting out your clothes, playing with your kids, decluttering the house, crawling back into bed. Isaiah 46:10 tells us we can "call the end from the beginning." That's what you are doing when you see the movie played out in your head before it's created in your life.

Step 5—Imagine the audience. Remember, you don't have to bear the burden of mastering your entire life. Just master today.

That's it. Just carry out your routines for 24 hours. Go ahead and imagine you have an audience. Imagine a crew is showing up to your house to film the reality show, Lifestyles of Rockstar Moms. You would show up dressed and prepped. You would have a plan for the day. You would have time for your kids and the energy to do everything you have to do, plus more. Why? People are watching! And this isn't just in your imagination. Whether you realize it, people are watching. There are women lined up who need a miracle and your success story will be the path that gets them there. It isn't all about you. Get your mind-set right, and the Momentum will follow.

Build the Ladder

Now it's time to boss up, Mama! We're going to create your routines—those little habits that will pull you out of the pit—day by day, rung by rung. There's no guessing here, either. My ladder ain't your ladder. That's why we're going to take your specific goals and turn them into routines to radically change your life. This is one of the vital parts of the Mom Mastery Method. The method works, but you've got to work the method. Ready for this?

Chapter 14: Reverse It Like a Rockstar

Have you ever gone into a room and forgotten why you went there? Join the club! It's all part of that Mom Fog that we're clearing out.

Once, I walked into the kitchen and opened up the fridge. There I was, staring into it with no clue as to what I was looking for. I then turned around and saw dishes piled in the sink so I put them in the dishwasher. While cleaning off the counters, I saw Kenna's book that I had previously told her to put away on the school shelf. I went outside to tell her to come put her book away when I noticed Korben had a cut on his foot. I went back inside to get some antibacterial wipes and a bandage. I went back outside and noticed some weeds taking over the flower bed so I pulled them out and placed them on the patio around the pool. After weeding, I went inside to get the broom to sweep off the patio. I grabbed the broom and went back outside. While sweeping, Klara asked how my book was coming along. This reminded me to get back inside my office to work on this book. When I returned to my desk I saw a tuna melt I had prepared for lunch, that had since cooled to room temperature. I took a bite and realized it would be a lot better with hot sauce. So I went to the kitchen and opened the fridge to get ... *(what I went there for in the first place)* ... the hot sauce!

If you give a mom a task, it's like giving a mouse a cookie. It just sets up a spiral that never ends and you don't get to enjoy the cookie! Instead of endless tasks, we're going to create routines.

We do this by switching gears from Drive to Reverse.

I could have spared myself all those distractions if I had opened the fridge and upon forgetting what I was looking for, just put myself in reverse. Go back to where I was and tend to what I was doing. Sometimes, working backwards is the best way to move forward. That's what we are doing in this chapter—creating your specific routines by reverse engineering!

When you reverse engineer, you look at the final product and then work backward: Break it down into the little steps you need to take and pieces you need to gather to create it. So, grab those INNER MOM goals, and let's break it down!

Final Product to First Steps

To reverse engineer your goals, take a good look at the final product and break your goals down into the yearly, monthly, weekly, and daily steps you need to take to reach them. Tony Robbins often says, "success leaves clues." Other people have achieved this success before. What did they do? What steps did they take? You don't have to invent the wheel. You just have to figure out how it's put together. This, you can totally do.

If it's a savings goal, how much do you want to save in a year? How much will you need to put aside each month? Each week?

If it's a decluttering goal, what rooms do you want to declutter? Can you do one a month? Can you spend 30 minutes a day on that room?

If it's a fitness goal, how can you get in shape? What type of exercise will you do? How often? For how long?

This can apply to every single goal, even the ones that are difficult to quantify. For example, if one of your goals is to have a better marriage, what steps can you take every day to encourage and support your spouse? A big sloppy kiss at the end of the day? A weekly backrub? A hot date night once a month?

You may look at your BFG goal and think, 'There's no way. I don't even know what steps I can take!' There are always steps you can take. Do you want to write a book? How about writing for one hour each morning? Do you want to build a business to seven figures? How about making 20 phone calls each weekday. Remember, God wants to do something miraculous in your life. All you have to do is "arise and walk," and let him open the doors along the path.

"A few years ago, I was addicted to Diet Coke (I carried at least one wherever I went, even to friends' homes). The days would fly by without much getting done, and end with the scramble to put dinner on the table. Today, two years into Mom Mastery University, the Diet Coke is out of my life. I have a meal plan for two weeks so I know what's for dinner, and my MAP allows me to seize the day, get everything done,

and still have time and energy to play with my kids and work on me! Life is an enjoyable walk, not a sprint. I have six kids and my husband travels a lot. MMU has given me the tools I need to feel alive and make the most out of my days."

—Erin R.

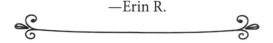

These steps will become your routines that you put into practice. No tough decision-making, no figuring out the process. Just simple routines. Put them into practice and they will shift to autopilot before you realize it! Write these routines down, and then we just MAP them out!

All the magic lies in the mundane. This is where we see it all come together! Bring out your MAP and let's stick those routines inside, and the more specific the better. Do you need to add a specific exercise regimen to your AM Routine? Do you need to create a specific time allotment to make calls or work on your budget? What about your spiritual growth? Can you set aside 30 minutes in the morning to devote to Bible reading and prayer? The little steps yield big results!

Now to Make Them Stick!

Remember that brain battle that is going on? One part of you is saying, "I want to do something new," and the other part is saying, "I want to stay where I am." That's totally cool. I got you. We are working on transforming your identity, because ultimately your identity forms your beliefs, and your beliefs form your behavior. These routines need a backbone, so keep doing your affirmations, enjoying your vision board, and thanking God for the eventual outcome.

However, that initial process of putting them into practice doesn't always feel so comfortable. You shifted gears from Drive to Reverse, and now you're shifting back into Drive. You'll be tempted to veer off at the closest rest stop. Keep in mind that it's the repetition of routines that is so important. That's why they're called "routines." Just keep doing them and eventually, they will become automatic. Eating one plate of nachos doesn't make you fat. It's eating one plate of nachos over and over and over. And making your bed once doesn't make you disciplined. It's making it over and over and over.

You can make these routines stick with some simple DOs and DON'Ts:

Do Set Your Stops / Don't Freestyle It.

You already know your routines need to be specific. But they also need to have a specific beginning and—most especially—an end. If you were a runner and didn't know how far a road race was going to be, would you enter it? Heck to the no! If you were a housepainter and didn't know how many walls you had to paint, would you start the project? Ain't happening! One huge reason we never start tasks is that we have no idea when (and if) we will ever finish them.

Don't try to freestyle these routines or you may land flat on your face. When you add them to your MAP, designate when you will stop each task. There are three types of stops. Pick the stop to match the routine, and you're set to go!

- Task Stop—Find one specific task to do from start to finish. Only assign a task stop when the task is something relatively small and you can accomplish it in less than 25 minutes. For example: Make a quick dinner, vacuum the floors, pay the bills, etc.

- Timed Stop—One of my favs! Set a specific amount of time to work on a task. When the time is up, you're done! There are a lot of clever ways to do this. You can set a timer on your phone, or create a playlist. When it was time to declutter my girls' closet, we put on the Trolls soundtrack. When it was over, we stopped. It really motivated all of us to put it in high gear and get the job done. (We may have repeated a couple of songs just so we could finish the entire job! And because it's a great soundtrack!).

- Tallied Stop—Set a number of tasks to do so you can divide a larger project into something more manageable. For example, my sister returned from a long vacation to find a huge stack of mail to go through. She decided to handle seven pieces of mail a day; that's it. She completely handled each piece. If it was a bill, she paid and filed it. If it was a letter, she answered it. In no time at all, her stack had disappeared.

Do Give Yourself Time / Don't Get Fast and Furious.

You didn't make a mess in a day, so why would you think you can clean it up in an hour? Chill, Mama. One of my clients had plugged into the Mom Mastery Method to lose weight and get her life in shape. After two months I talked with her to see how she was doing. She was disappointed because she had only lost 30 pounds. Yes! Disappointed!

I said, "So, you spent the last four decades abusing your body and you're frustrated because you haven't reached your goal weight in two months?"

She realized that she needed to be more realistic in her expectations, as well as to celebrate her success. Energy flows where your attention goes. If she had stayed focused on the weight she had NOT lost, her body would have continued to hold onto it. By celebrating the healthy body she was creating, she gives herself permission to let go of the extra weight. Remember, it's never about circumstances. It's about the identity that creates the belief that creates the behavior that creates the circumstances. Get the identity right, and everything flows from there.

"I love having more energy now to get my day going! Applying the Mom Mastery Method and having a vision of ABUNDANCE has changed my routines of how I manage my time

and money!"

—Gloria R.

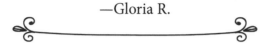

Give yourself time. Remember, transforming your identity is always the first step, and that takes a while. You are also growing in places you can't see right now. It can get frustrating. Changes start out so small and insignificant. Saving $50 a month doesn't seem like all that much until you look at it way down the road. The little routines really do add up in huge ways. Be patient and know your faith is at work. And faith is the substance of things hoped for. It's the evidence of things you can't see yet (Hebrews 11:1). Just keep plugging along.

Do Reward Yourself / Don't Be a Mommy Martyr.

When your attempts go unrewarded, you eventually give up. That predicament is called Learned Helplessness, and it's at the core of Mom Fatigue Syndrome. Nothing you do is working and you feel helpless, frustrated, and exhausted. That's why it is extremely important to reward yourself. Hey, if no one is going to pat you on the back, then wrap your arms around yourself and pat away, Mama!

Rewards are necessary to keep us going. It's just the way the brain functions. Give the mouse a cookie, for crying out loud. Just make sure that mouse has done her routine and she can sit and enjoy it! For my body's sake, I try to steer clear of using food as a reward. Remember, rewards don't have to be big. Just little tokens to give your inner mom the clear message that you did the job and did it well. Here are some examples:

Flavored seltzer water after I finish my afternoon work period.
Plugging in my decorative lights after I've picked up my office.
Green smoothie after my AM Routine.
Lighting a candle after I clean up the kitchen.
Strolling out to the dock for a breather after all the laundry is put away.
Manicure after a week of hard work and completing all tasks.
Starbucks coffee on Sunday afternoon if I met my weekly goals.

See? They're not huge. Just little winks you give yourself to say, "You got this!" Jessica, one of the moms inside Mom Mastery University, started a workout program and bought a new calendar and a book of star stickers to keep her going. She would put a sticker on each day she exercised. If she exercised at least 5 days a week, she would buy herself a new piece of workout clothing for her wardrobe. Hey, we never grow out of shiny gold stars!

Do Use Your Phone / Don't Abuse Your Phone

Your phone is a tool; a fantastic tool! But just like any tool, you can use it to build or to destroy. Check it out:

"Every wise woman builds her house, but the foolish one tears it down with her own hands" (Proverbs 14:1 AMPC).

If you are like most moms, you have your phone within hand's reach all day long. The King James Version of that verse says, "Every wise woman buildeth her house: but the foolish plucketh it down with her hands." You don't need a hammer or saw in your hands to build up or tear down your home. You can do it with your phone.

"The Mom Mastery Method literally changed my life. Implementing the routines into my life leaves space for me to get out of the debilitating decision fatigue and clears my mind to be able to think. This gives me energy and vitality to be able to conquer the day! Before I learned this method, I would literally wake up still tired from the day before!"

—Semalee B.

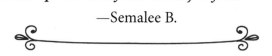

You are building your home from the inside-out. You are creating your legacy and designing your destiny. You can use your phone to create an energizing playlist while you clean your house, keep up with your MAP, and set alarms to coincide with your routines. Or you can use your phone to mindlessly scroll on Instagram and play games to win imaginary tokens. Your legacy is way more valuable than token graphics. Use your phone to help push your routines forward, not as a distraction to hold you back.

Do Add One Routine Each Day / Don't Overwhelm Yourself.

I started by folding my laundry. That's it. After that, I started making my bed. Then I added picking out my clothes, then meal planning, then paying off debt, and more. If I had tried to do everything at once, I would have jumped ship long before seeing any results.

Inch by inch, life's a cinch. Yard by yard, life is hard. Mile by mile, you end up hospitalized! We're not doing 50-yard dashes here. We're creating abundant, energetic, joyful lives—step by step.

Go ahead and break down your goals into routines. Then add them to your MAP, one day at a time. This is where a day planner or calendar helps tremendously. You can plot out your incremental growth.

I have also included the "21-Day Rockin' Routine Challenge" to help you along the path. Incorporate six new routines—one each day—for an entire week. Take one day off, continuing to do those previous routines but not adding any new ones, then repeat. This is an incremental program that will build up over three weeks. This is just an example. You can change it around and make it more specific to suit your personal goals.

21-Day Rockin' Routine Challenge

Day 1: Make Up Your Bed

Making your bed is such a great way to start practicing personal discipline. You may think it doesn't matter because no one will see, but God rewards in public what we do in private. One way to incorporate rewards for this routine is to purchase or make a scented linen spray you can spritz on your sheets before you make up your bed. It will make crawling in at night so much better.

Still not convinced? U.S. Navy Admiral William H. McCraven, in a speech given to the graduates of his alma mater, the University of Texas in Austin, said, "If you want to change the world, start off by making your bed." He continued with, "If you make your bed every morning, you will have accomplished the first task of the day. It will give you a small sense of pride, and it will encourage you to do another task, and another, and another. And by the end of the day that one task completed will have turned into many tasks completed."

It's true. The little things build the big things. Never underestimate the power of routines, and the power of a made-up bed!

Day 2: Wake Up to an Alarm

Many moms let the day wake them up—crying baby, kids needing breakfast, phone ringing. No more! You are going to wake up the day and take it by storm! Do this by setting an alarm and waking up before anyone else. I know this can be difficult with young children, but if you are going to execute an AM Routine, you must do this. Plus, you will go into the day feeling powerful and productive! One way to help with this routine is to use a motivating song as your phone alarm. Choose one that inspires you! I've used songs like:

Happy by Pharrell Williams
Firework by Katy Perry
Blessed by Brett Dennen
It's On by Superchick
Greatest Day by Bowling for Soup

Day 3: Create Your Calendar

If you are not using a day planner, start now. As part of my PM Routine, I look over my plans for the next day to make sure I am fully prepared and ready to execute them. Even if you think you're going to leave most of it blank, it will help to just start your day planner and begin using it to write down your routines. Once you start this habit, you'll wonder how you ever got along without it. You can use a day planner that works with your specific style. You may prefer an app on your phone, or the old-school method—pen and paper. I have a perfect day planner system, along with video tutorials and downloadable planner sheets, at hannahhelpme.com/planner.

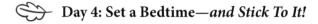 **Day 4: Set a Bedtime—*and Stick To It!***

One of the best ways to feel more energized during the day is to get more sleep at night. Your body and your brain need it desperately! But, here's the problem—moms don't often have down time because of the constant pushing and pulling by someone or something. Often, we use time at night to just sit and NOT BE NEEDED (that's where you say, "Amen!"). This becomes screen time when lots of mindless online surfing happens. And guess what—that's totally okay. Your brain needs a period of "mindlessness." However, you need to set stops with this as well as any other routine, because with mindless activity like this, minutes can quickly bleed into hours. Give yourself 25 minutes to just surf online or watch television, or color, or look through magazines. Then stop! Turn off the TV or computer and get your butt to bed!

If sleeping is hard to come by, then incorporate relaxation techniques into your PM Routine. These may include a cup of chamomile tea, a warm bath, soft stretches, or maybe diffusing some calming oils in your bedroom.

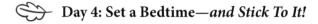 **Day 5: Lay Out Your Clothes**

How much time and energy have you wasted in the morning trying to find something to wear? As part of your PM Routine, lay out the outfit you are going to wear the next day, along with any accessories, such as jewelry.

Wait, jewelry? Hannah, I'm a mom!

Darn right, you're a mom. It's the greatest career in the world so treat it with the respect it deserves. Show up as a professional, and you'll get professional results.

ᗡᗡ Day 6: Practice Meditation

Meditation? Isn't that a little "woo woo?"

Not at all! You are already meditating, so why not use it to your advantage? Meditation is merely concentrated focus. Do you ever worry? That's meditation, just in a negative direction. Jesus went away to pray and meditate, so let's follow His example. Take time in the morning, as part of your AM Routine, to just sit and spend time in God's presence. This is a great time to practice gratitude, which is the attitude of abundance. Gratitude will attract so many wonderful things into your life.

If you are new to meditation or a bit skeptical about it, no problem. STEP SEVEN: MEDITATION will take care of all that.

ᗡᗡ Day 7: Rest Day—Practice Your Routines

ᗡᗡ Day 8: Eat Breakfast

Too often, we hit the ground running with little more than a cup of coffee in our systems. Your brain and your body need some healthy fuel! You certainly don't have to give up your cup of coffee but make it healthier and make that energy last longer by adding collagen powder for protein and some MCT oil, which is great brain food.

In addition to your coffee, consider consuming something with more staying power so you don't mentally and physically drop off later. Try a healthy green smoothie recipe and or some other nutritious concoction.

Once, I was in a hurry to leave the house and stumbled upon one of my favorite morning mocha recipes. All we had was cold coffee from the day before and I didn't even have time to warm it up. I poured the cold coffee into my shaker bottle, along with almond milk, chocolate protein and greens powder, some collagen, and a squirt of MCT oil. It was fabulous and kept me energized and focused all morning long.

Day 9: Plan Your Meals

This simple routine will save you boatloads of time, money, and energy. Just get a small calendar you can post in your home and write down your monthly menu on it. Now at first you may think that's way too difficult. But, hold on, Mama. You know by now I've got your back. You can certainly come up with 20 meals, right? Think about the different meals you serve now and get the family to help you. They will have plenty of great ideas.

When you collect 20 meal ideas, you can basically fill out the entire month. On Saturdays, we do "YOYO" meals, which means "You're On Your Own." And on Sundays, the whole family comes over and we grill out, have a taco fiesta, or share a big pot of soup. Also, when you plan out a week's worth of meals you almost always have leftovers on the weekend.

The best news about this routine? You only have to do it once! Plan out one really good month, then just repeat it! You don't have to come up with brand-new meal ideas each month. Just put it on a cycle.

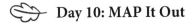 Day 10: MAP It Out

As part of your PM Routine, spend a few minutes looking over your MAP for the next day. You will get mentally prepared for everything you need to do, and will be sure to have everything you need so there are no surprises.

If you plan to make a slow-cooker meal the next day, you can make sure you have all the ingredients. If you're going to the library, you can get all the books together. If you're teaching a new subject, you can look over the materials. If you're making some new calls, you can prepare client profiles. Save the surprises for birthday parties. A prepared mom is a happy mom!

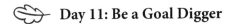 Day 11: Be a Goal Digger

Find your top 5 INNER MOM goals—those that hit your biggest

pain or pleasure points. These are your "Fab 5." Each morning and evening, as part of your AM and PM Routines, write down the Fab 5. That's all. Just write them down.

A recent study found that you become 42 percent more likely to achieve your goals and dreams, simply by writing them down on a regular basis. When you think about your goals, you activate the right hemisphere of your brain: the imagination center. But when you write down your goals, you then tap into the power of the left hemisphere: the logical side. Suddenly, both hemispheres are firing. It's like every neuron and cell in your mind and body are screaming, "This is my reality and I mean it!"

Day 12: Drink Your Water

Dehydration is one of the main causes of fatigue. To determine how much water you should be drinking, take your weight and divide it in half. That is how many ounces you should drink each day. For example, a 160-lb. woman should drink 80 ounces of water, which is 10 cups (1 cup = 8 ounces).

With our very full lifestyles, it's not always easy to remember to drink our water, so just turn it into a routine. If you need 10 cups, set five alarms during the day to drink 2 cups. You can also make it more enjoyable by adding slices of lemon or cucumber, or herbal tea bags.

Day 13: Make Your House Shine

Your housekeeping needs to be a routine as well. It should be a sprint, not a marathon. We spend more energy thinking about cleaning than we do cleaning. It really doesn't require that much time and energy, just short routines you can create in two steps:

Step 1—Write down all your daily and weekly housekeeping chores, like emptying trash, laundry, vacuuming, etc. Then divide them among five days. You can even download the "Chore Chart" with a video tutorial at hannahkeeley.com/chorechart. Add a set amount of time to do your chores, about an hour, into your MAP.

Step 2—For deep cleaning and decluttering, tackle it in zones. Divide your home into four zones:

Zone 1:	Kitchen, Dining Room, Pantry
Zone 2:	Living Areas, Play Room
Zone 3:	Bathrooms, Bedrooms
Zone 4:	Yard, Porch, Garage

For each week in a month, designate one week to tackle each zone. Add an extra 30-minute slot to your MAP each day to do your deep cleaning and decluttering; and remember to take baby steps and set your stops. It will be done in no time. Each month, I offer a free Crazy Calendar that does all the scheduling for you. Make sure you download your monthly calendar by going to hannahkeeley.com/crazycalendar

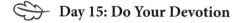 **Day 14: Rest Day—Practice Your Routines**

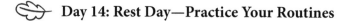 **Day 15: Do Your Devotion**

You know by now that God is your Source, so don't start the day without Him. Incorporate a daily devotion as part of your AM Routine. Don't get wrapped up in finding the perfect devotional. Just use your Bible and let the Holy Spirit be your Teacher. Spend time reading the Word and talking with Him in prayer. If you don't know where to start, I have the perfect Bible reading program made for moms called, "The Short Attention Span Bible Reading Program." You can get free access to it at www.biblesquirrel.com

Day 16: Move That Body

You don't need to be a gym rat to reap the benefits of exercise. Your body just needs to move. That's what God made it for! Today is when you establish a daily exercise routine. Set aside 30 minutes on your MAP to elevate your heart and get your glow on! You can also do this routine with the kids. They will love dancing to oldies, going walking, or biking around the neighborhood. You can always increase the intensity later. For now, just get moving.

One mom who went through this challenge was unable to exercise because of her physical condition. She started with 30 minutes of stretching and moving in her chair. This led to her being able to lose weight, get more energy, and increase her mobility. There is always something you can do to honor that temple God has given you.

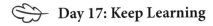 **Day 17: Keep Learning**

We live in such a rich time of learning opportunities. You can listen to and learn from tons of awesome podcasts and audible books. You can even pair this routine with another physical activity. For example, each morning when I do my hair and makeup, I listen to a sermon or podcast.

Moms are also behind the wheel—a lot! A study by the University of Southern California found that if you drive 12,000 miles a year, you can get the equivalent of two years of college education in three years' time just by listening to educational information while driving.

Think about the areas where you want to grow, and start listening to learn. You have access to the wisdom of the world at the touch of your fingertip. Use it! I have transformed my life, my home, my business, and my family by listening to audio books, podcasts, and sermons.

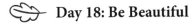 **Day 18: Be Beautiful**

Putting your best face forward changes your attitude tremendously! You're already beautiful, but just spending 5-10 minutes fixing your hair and putting on a little makeup radically changes how you approach your career as a mom. Even if you don't wear makeup, just styling your hair and swiping on some lip gloss and perfume tell the world (and yourself) that you're ready for anything!

Rozanna, one of our Mom Mastery University students went through the 21-Day Rockin' Routine Challenge and had never worn makeup. The day she incorporated this routine, her little boy saw her walk in his room that morning and said, "Mommy, why are you so pretty?" She replied, "For you!" She wrote me a letter telling me what an impact this one simple routine made on her and her children. With a swipe of lip gloss and a bit of mascara, she demonstrated to her family how much she valued them and her role as their mother. I'm telling you, those bottles and tubes are powerful!

Day 19: Prep Your Meals

You already planned your meals. Now it's time to incorporate the routine of prepping them. Don't let dinnertime surprise you. You know it's coming. It does every single day. Create a routine of getting in the kitchen and putting love, care, and positive energy into preparing your meals.

Many families pray before meals, but if you are the one preparing the meal, I would suggest you pray before you do that as well. Prayer changes things. Prayer brings healing power to the food and a loving spirit into the kitchen.

Several studies have shown that when emotions were projected onto food, the food began to assume those qualities. For example, Dr. Masaru Emoto did an experiment where he said "Thank you" to one bowl of rice, and "You are a fool" to the other. After 30 days, the "thank you" rice was beginning to nicely ferment and give off a lovely aroma. The "fool" rice was moldy and rotten. No words are idle. They are seeds and will always produce fruit, good or bad.

Once I was worried about a situation while I was in the kitchen preparing breakfast. My oldest daughter commented, "Mom, this oatmeal doesn't taste right. Were you in a bad mood when you made it?" She could taste the worry in the food!

Your emotions and your words are so powerful. Use that power in the kitchen when you prepare meals, even if it's just a simple pot of oatmeal. It's an easy routine to establish and maintain.

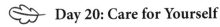 Day 20: Care for Yourself

Across the board, moms are guilty of not caring for themselves enough. Inside Mom Mastery University (MMU), it's mandatory that our students dedicate the last Friday of every month to self-care. Moms often put themselves last on the list. They're at the bottom of the totem pole, while all the weight they are bearing is crushing them.

You are a precious gift to this world, and you need to care for yourself appropriately. If you're not filled up, you can't give anything to those people you love the most. Create a routine of caring for yourself. Dedicate one day a month, like we do at MMU, or maybe make it a weekly thing. It doesn't have to be extravagant. Sometimes, it's just a cup of tea, a bubble bath, and a facial mask. Or maybe coloring and watching a favorite movie. My sister sets aside one day a month to get her nails done. My neighbor goes to a weekly Zumba class. I indulge in a cup of Starbucks coffee once a week. This is your self-care, so make it what you want.

The important thing about self-care is that you do it intentionally. Don't grab a cup of coffee while you're out running errands and think, 'I'll just count this as my self-care.' Do it on purpose. Plan for it. Get excited about it. You deserve it!

Establish a routine of self-care and do it with ZERO guilt! When you care for yourself, you are also caring for every member of your family. They need you operating at 100 percent, and you can't do this if you're sputtering on fumes. This routine will serve you and everyone else you love.

Day 21: Practice Your Routines and Keep Practicing Them!

The important thing about routines, is that you do them routinely! Put them on a loop in your life, and they will work wonders. You create your routines, then your routines create you. Here's to the very best you!

Go to www.rockinroutine.com
to get your free online 21-Day Rockin Routine challenge.

STEP SEVEN: MEDITATION

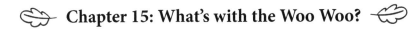 ## Chapter 15: What's with the Woo Woo?

I'm embarrassed to even go back to that day.

The scent of sage hung heavy in the air and a thin man with a long ponytail sat cross-legged in a white suit in front of the class. The suit was a loose-fitting number. It looked like the love child of a karate gi and a bathrobe, the kind of suit that screamed, "Yo! I'm comfortable, I'm confident, and I'm the perfect outfit to wear to a buffet restaurant."

The room was dark except for one candle resting on the floor in front of the man who called himself a yogi. I smiled and nodded my head when he first told me his title, because I thought he was talking about a bear. He wasn't. A yogi is evidently a big deal. But then again, so is a bear—especially if you're hiking and you accidentally run into one.

But I digress.

Everyone in the room was sitting cross-legged like Mr. Yogi, including myself. Then, without warning, he picked up a small mallet with one hand and hit a miniature gong which he was holding in his other hand. Taking a deep breath, and matching the key in perfect pitch, he then began to loudly chant, "Ommmm ..."

Then something horrible happened. It was the worst. Like THE worst. In fact, I feel so terrible even sharing this.

I … I giggled.

It just erupted out of my mouth—a teeny, tiny little laugh. I couldn't help it. This was my first experience "meditating" (as Mr. Yogi referred to it), and I don't even know why it happened. Everything just felt so weird at the time and here was a Yogi hitting a gong and doing a baritone "*Pitch Perfect*" thing. I had no idea what was going on, so I just reacted in the only way I knew how.

I giggled.

Evidently, you never giggle during meditation. I realized that when every head in the room turned to me and I saw an array of scowling faces looking in my direction. Faces that seemed to say, "You wouldn't know what to do with a gong if it hit you over the head!"

I had evidently committed the unpardonable sin of meditation, and didn't even realize it. Mr. Yogi opened his eyes, wrinkled up his nose, and gave me a sort of smirk, the kind of face grown-ups make when a toddler accidentally smears melted chocolate all over their white sofa.

"I'm so sorry," I said. "I'm just really new at this."

Mr. Yogi nodded and simply said, "All is well. Let's try to focus," and started over with the gong stuff.

All I wanted to do was shrink down to the size of a sage leaf and float out the window. I was obviously not destined to live the life of a Yogi, which was a bit disappointing since I was thinking those love child outfits would look pretty good on me, or at least allow me access to unlimited yeast rolls.

'That's it,' I thought to myself. 'I'm never doing this again.'

I was so wrong. I didn't realize it at the time, but I was actually meditating every day of my life. And I still do. And, guess what— so do you!

Everybody Meditates

If you want to burn sage and bang a gong, then get it on. If you want to sit on the sofa and chill, that's cool, too. The truth is, everyone already meditates. The only problem is that most people are doing it all wrong.

Meditation is thinking deeply or focusing one's mind for a period of time. Somehow, over the course of modern history, we began to think of meditation as a funky "woo woo" mystical New Age experience. When it's really just deep, focused thinking. And everybody does that.

'Hannah, you don't know me. I can't focus for longer than two minutes.'

You're preaching to the preacher, Mama. But, let's hit "pause" for a minute. Have you ever laid awake at night worrying about something—a rebellious kid, a medical diagnosis, a job situation, or a bill you couldn't pay? If you have, then you already know how to meditate, because that's exactly what you were doing. Have you ever had a situation in your life that you couldn't "get off your mind?" If that's ever happened, you were meditating like a yogi! Meditation isn't a difficult practice. You've been doing it your whole life. Meditation is just focused thinking, which can be positive or negative. Learn how to do it right and put the power of meditation to work for you instead of against you!

Nothing "New Age" About It!

Many people hear the word "meditation" and they think it's a New Age principle. Far from it. Meditation is prayer. Prayer is meditation. And Abraham was one heck of a praying man. In fact, he was always going around talking to God, about anything and everything. In Genesis 24:63 we find out that "… Isaac went out to meditate and bow down [in prayer] in the open country in the evening …" (AMPC). Where did he learn meditation from? He saw his daddy, Abraham, doing it routinely.

And that's the trick—meditating and praying as a daily routine. But before we can DO meditation, we need to find out why we DON'T DO meditation.

Let me ask you a question. If you knew there was an all-natural supplement you could take each day that would magically boost your physical and mental health, and it was free, would you take it? Heck yeah! Sign me up for auto-ship! Many people, especially us moms, tend to brush off meditation for one of two reasons— it's a waste or it's weird.

"Since I was a teenager the first thought I had every morning was, 'I NEED coffee! Now, after implementing the Mom Mastery Method I often forget to even make coffee because I'm so in charge of my day the moment I wake up! Also, when other mamas complain of being too tired for Mom's Night Out, my response: Cannot relate!"

—Amanda K.

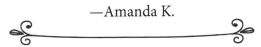

Instead of a waste, meditation is most likely to be one of the best uses of your time each day. God talks a lot about "first fruits" offering. Giving the first of your harvest back to God isn't just an Old Testament rule. It's a way of living. Romans 11:16 tells us that if the first piece of dough is holy, the whole lump is, too. And when you dedicate the first of your day to God, the rest goes a whole lot better. Meditation is a way to set your mind and prime yourself to create your very best day. Awesome days don't happen by accident; they are strategically crafted. And the great news is that if you learn to create one, you can create another, and another, and soon you have it down to a science. As a mom, you give a whole lot of yourself, so it's best to start the day with a full tank. Meditation helps you do that.

As far as the whole "weird" thing goes, our culture just made it that way. As usual, God created something for our benefit and the world twists it around and messes it up. God gave us apples; the world makes Apple Jacks. God gave us meditation; the world adds gongs and incense. Meditation with God is extraordinarily beneficial. But meditation without God, well, yeah. That can get weird. Truth is, God created us to meditate. We do it already. But if you're not making it intentional, it becomes destructive.

It's Got Its Perks

Meditation benefits your body in amazing ways—physically and mentally. Check out the short list:

It increases immune function.

It decreases inflammation.

It alleviates pain.

It decreases depression.

It decreases anxiety.

It lowers blood pressure.

It reduces stress.

It slows the aging process.

It improves concentration.

It improves the ability to focus.

It increases overall happiness.

It improves memory.

It increases brain matter.

It improves the ability to multi-task.

Yeah, that's the short list! Are you sold yet? I'm sure every mom out there needs all the above (especially that "reduces stress" bullet point!). Meditation has remarkable benefits, not just for your mind and your body, but on a spiritual level as well. It's a tool that can help you in the present, and can also help you create the life you want to live in the future.

Just like awesome days don't happen by accident, awesome lives don't either. You need to use the force of faith to pull that kind of awesomeness together. And meditation gives you a tool to tap into that force. I like to imagine it like this. Let's say you're at Point A and your awesome life is at Point B. By using the Mom Mastery Method, you are making progress toward Point B. But by adding Meditation, you also are causing your awesome life (Point B) to make progress toward you (Point A). Meditation doubles the speed of manifestation. You're moving toward abundance, while abundance is moving toward you. Meditation is way too powerful to overlook. In other words, do NOT skip this step.

Be Imitators of God

Meditation helps you tap into the force of faith. In Hebrews 11:3, we find out that "By faith we understand that the worlds [during the successive ages] were framed (fashioned, put in order, and equipped for their intended purpose) by the word of God, so that what we see was not made out of things which are visible" (AMPC).

God had to speak it before He could create it. And God had to think it before He could speak it. That's why it says that what we see was not made out of the visible, but the invisible. Everything had to begin as a thought. Everything was created in the spiritual realm before it was created in the physical realm. Not just with God, but with us as well.

In Ephesians 5:1 we are called to be "imitators of God." The way He does things is how we do things. How he acts is how we act. He creates in the spiritual and it is then manifested in the physical. When He created this world, He thought it first. He imagined it, focused on it, and thought out all the details; then He spoke it and it was!

We follow the same recipe. We must create the day in the spiritual realm before it can manifest in the physical. Meditation allows us to create our day before we live it. One day is a powerful tool. Don't go swinging into it like a wrecking ball. Take time to imagine it, focus on it, and think out the details. Call the end from the beginning!

Dandelions vs Wheat

According to God's Word we are supposed to live by faith (Hebrews 10:38). We're also supposed to walk by faith (2 Corinthians 5:7). But how can we live it out and walk it out if we don't even know what "it" is? For many people, faith is a cool post on Instagram or a trivial word we throw around when times get tough. But it's so much more. It's the power we have available to us to operate under the grace of God to create our reality. And the big news is—you are already using it. The current condition of your life reveals how you have used this creative force.

Okay, I know things just got a bit heavy there, so let me break it down for you; because you absolutely, positively must get this concept! It took me over four decades to understand this. But as soon as I really got it, that's when my life began to turn around. That's when my income changed, my home changed, my health changed—everything changed.

"I've just begun meditating, and already I'm feeling more grounded. My favorite part was learning that I don't have to empty my mind. Whatever thoughts surface, I hold them, look at them objectively and ask for wisdom from God. It's such a peaceful experience, and then I'm ready for the day!"

—Nancy E.

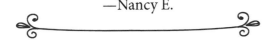

It's like you're planting acres and acres of seed every season of your life and begging God for a harvest of wheat, when the only things that ever come out of the ground are dandelions. Then one day, you decide to look at the bags of seeds you've been planting and realize they all have labels that read, "Dandelions." You slap yourself upside the head, throw out those seeds, order wheat seeds on Amazon Prime, get them delivered to your front door in 20 minutes, and waste no time getting those beauties in the ground so you can finally start enjoying the harvest you've been praying for! It won't happen overnight, but you have complete confidence that it will happen eventually, even by next harvest season.

That's why the Bible refers to faith as "seed" so many times. Because the truth is with every thought you hold in your head and every word that exits your mouth, you are planting something. So, let's do some Spiritual Botany 101. It's as easy as 1-2-3.

1. Understand that meditation is seed, and you already meditate. Thoughts become things. It's truly as simple—*and as complicated*—as that. You are already planting seeds in the ground. I could visit you for 24 hours and tell you exactly what thoughts you meditated on one year earlier. You need to take a critical look at your life right now and see the harvest that is already growing. No excuses, no rationalizing. Just a tough, gut-punchin' look at the harvest.

2. Realize you are looking into the past. When you take that hard look, and your life is not exactly in the shape you want it in, give yourself some grace. You are not looking at who you are. You are looking at who you were. Big, fat difference. Don't get discouraged with the unpaid bills or the cluttered bedroom, or the irritating kids. That's just a look into the past, a view of the dandelion field. Get excited that you are using the Mom Mastery Method to plant new seeds and create a new harvest. God makes all things new (Revelation 21:5) and He is doing a brand-new thing in you (Isaiah 43:19). Give yourself grace, and time.

3. Put the power of meditation to work for you. This is how we change the seeds we're planting. Focusing your thoughts in a positive direction and communicating with a God Who wants the best for you are powerful ways to get the right seeds in the ground and harvest what you really want in life.

The Unfair Advantage

Have you ever been to therapy? Ever paid out the nose for a counseling session? Once, I paid $2,500 for a one-hour counseling session one afternoon with my business coach. You better know that when 2 p.m. rolled around I was sitting at my computer with my screen open and my pen ready! My kids were glued to Harry Potter with strict instructions (threats) not to interrupt me.

When it comes to prayer and meditation, you have an open invitation for the most productive counseling session you could ever imagine. The only problem is that we don't value it as much. I've signed up for plenty of online business workshops and trainings and (being totally honest here) whether I attend or not depends on how much I paid for them. If they're free, even though they may include great information, my perception of the value is distorted. I didn't put anything in, so I probably won't get anything out. If something comes up and I can't make it, no big deal. But when I have skin in the game, I'm going to make that appointment! It's just how the human brain operates. If we don't invest anything in something, we don't value it. And if we don't value it, we don't execute it.

That's often the problem with prayer. It's an amazingly valuable counseling session. But it's free, so our perception of the value is distorted. Jesus paid the price for us so we don't have to. He died to give us access to this holy counseling session. After His resurrection, the disciples wanted Him to chill with them a little longer. But He explained it this way:

"… I tell you the truth: It is expedient for you that I go away. For if I do not go away, the Counselor will not come to you. But if I go, I will send Him to you. When He comes…He will guide you into all truth. For He will not speak on His own authority. But He will speak whatever He hears, and He will tell you things that are to come. He will glorify Me, for He will receive from Me and will declare it to you. All that the Father has is Mine. Therefore I said that He will take what is Mine and will declare it to you" (John 16:7-8;13-15 MEV).

He also told us the Counselor was there to help us! "But the Helper (Comforter, Advocate, Intercessor—Counselor, Strengthener, Standby), the Holy Spirit, whom the Father will send in My name [in My place, to represent Me and act on My behalf], He will teach you all things. And He will help you remember everything that I have told you" (John 14:26 AMP).

"I have 5 kids, some with higher needs, and before being introduced to the Mom Mastery Method I was exhausted and overwhelmed in every area of life. I worked HARD but

couldn't ever reach my goals. I was chasing my tail all the time. I didn't know how to take care of myself or my family without completely exhausting myself and going through cycles of insane busyness that produced NOTHING and crashing from exhaustion and defeat. I tried everything. Since using this method, I have more energy than I thought possible. I'm free from overwhelm and mom guilt, and I'm reaching my goals so quickly I have to keep coming up with new ones!"

—Rachel P.

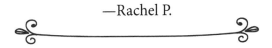

Our Counselor is the Holy Spirit. When Jesus left the earth, He sent the Holy Spirit to dwell in us, to help, comfort, strength, counsel us, and so much more. So many times, moms think that if Jesus were just sitting beside them on the sofa and could tell them what to do, life would be so much easier. But according to Jesus, we have something even better—the Holy Spirit. He's not sitting beside us. He is dwelling within us!

God doesn't want us groping and grinding through life. He wants to give His kids an "unfair advantage." That's what the Holy Spirit does. He counsels us through life to avoid the potholes, maneuver the obstacles, and take the shortcuts. It's like 24/7 access to the wisdom to win in life. After all, God knows more than we do; and thankfully, He wants to share His knowledge with us. And He does it through His Word and prayer.

Prayer isn't for God's benefit. It's for ours. In Psalm 119:97-98, we learn that meditation makes us wiser than our enemies. You've got plenty of enemies, Mama—stress, bills, relationship struggles, clutter, health issues; shall I go on? Meditation makes you wiser than your enemies, so you can know how to do battle and win. It's the counseling session to beat all counseling sessions. But you gotta show up!

Your Power Source

Your phone died. Again.

We've all been there. Once I was right in the middle of a live video and my phone powered down. Yup, that's what happens when you don't charge it up. We know that about our phones, but we forget that when it comes to our spirits. Your life is at stake here, and you need to stay plugged in to your power source. Don't you feel better coming out of a kick-butt counseling session? You're refreshed, armed, and ready. You're powered up.

Jesus said, "If you remain in me and I in you, you will bear much fruit; apart from me you can do nothing" (John 15:5 NIV). Giving the world a time-out and stepping into prayer is your way of charging up. You can be busy and spin your wheels, or be fruitful and live in abundance. You choose. Don't get fooled into thinking that the busier you are, the worthier you are. Jesus has already made you worthy. You don't need to prove anything, especially to yourself.

"It's an MMU testimony! I reworked our daily schedule and started speaking character proclamations over my sweet daughter. On Wednesday we saw a huge improvement. She was running up to my hubby when he got home. Never done that before! So hubby told me whatever I'm doing keep it up. Last night she was in his lap giggling with him. He said this is a completely different child! Praise the Lord!"
—Brenda S.

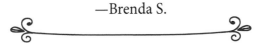

As moms, our pride often makes purchases that our energy can't pay. To combat the low self-esteem we often feel in our roles as moms, we will fill our plates full and run around like a bunch of crazy gerbils on crack, hustling our buns but getting nothing done. We just put out fire after fire after fire. But prayer stops that. It's our first fruits offering of the day to step back into our purpose and fuel up with wisdom. It's our "unfair advantage" that gives us the solutions to problems we don't even have yet. Instead of spending our days putting out fires, we take the time to become fireproof!

But if you're anything like me, you like steps. You like the breakdown. You have enough complication in your life, and the thought of bringing more mess into the picture is just not on the horizon. The good news? Meditation isn't messy. In the next chapter, I'll show you how to make it a super simple and immensely gratifying part of your day.

Chapter 16: Meditation for MVPs and Other Non-Yogis

My husband's grandfather was a true-blue cowboy. He traveled all over with the rodeo, dazzling spectators with his ability to rope calves, ride bulls, walk with a swagger, and all those other things that cowboys do. He was a cowboy from head to toe, from his hat to his spurs. He was the real deal.

But just because he could ride a bull, didn't mean he could run with them. Two totally different things!

If you could compare your daily life to meditation, it would be like comparing bull riding to running with the bulls. I'm sure you've seen the footage, or maybe you've experienced, the bull run in Pamplona. A lot of bulls run through the city while people test their own endurance, strength, speed, and, evidently, common sense by running with them. I don't have to run with bulls. I'm a mom. That's close enough.

Running with the bulls is like your daily life. It's chaotic, a thousand things are going on around you that are potential threats, and it's moving at a frantic pace. Bull riding is like meditation. It's a challenge, but in a different way. It's a learned skill and it requires every bit of your focus in one singular direction. And for a mom, it is often one of the most difficult steps of the Mom Mastery Method because of how our MVP brains are wired. But I wouldn't put you on a bull the first day of the rodeo, so we're going to take this whole meditation thing step by step. You already know the "why" of meditation; now let's get to the "how." Strap on them spurs, Darlin'. Time to ride that bull!

Pinterest Prayer

One way to break down prayer is to talk about what it's not. We all like it when something can be neatly arranged in a Pinterest post or simplified to 140 characters. We like simple tasks that we can scratch off our list. Prayer is no exception. But in all the pretty Pinterest posts, you never see the mess behind the scenes. There's the pretty avocado toast on the antique china plate. But where's the ugly blackish-green peel and the pit with the knife stuck in it and all the bread crumbs around the toaster? The thing about prayer is that it can't always be "pinned." God is enough to receive all of you—the good, the bad, and the ugly, with a tint of blackish-green.

"It would have been amazing if they taught this stuff in college or even high school! I came across Hannah years ago and so grateful that God guided her to create this amazing university transforming motherhood one mom at a time!"
—Jennifer K.

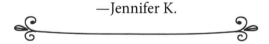

I went to a private Christian high school and had to take a Bible class. That class almost ruined my spiritual walk—seriously. It was so steeped in religion and rules and bondage, that me and

Jesus almost didn't make it out alive. One lesson we learned was "how to pray." My teacher instructed us to pray using the ACTS formula—Adoration, Confession, Thanksgiving, and Supplication. I came home from school that day feeling horrible because I thought I had been doing prayer all wrong. So instead of just chilling with the JC, I began making prayer a formal ritual.

Me (in my head, as a teenage girl): *'Okay, here we go. Dear God— let me see, A, that stands for adoration. Umm, God? I really love you. I adore you. You're great. Okay, C. Confession. Okay, well, I guess I was really horrible in some way today. Oh, yeah, I cheated on that science quiz ... So ... I guess I confess that. But that was pretty brilliant how I wrote the answers on the bottom of my shoe. Please still help me get an "A," okay? And, let's see. What's next? Oh yeah, T. Thanksgiving. Thank You so much, God, for my family and my health, and all that good stuff. And, oh crap. What was the last one? Oh, wait. I said "crap." I need to go back to Confession. God, please forgive me for saying, "crap." Um. Dang it. What's next? Supplication! Yeah! That's it! God, please supply all the cool stuff that I want. Like David, the soccer player. He's so hot. Yes, him. I'll take that. Oh, and don't let Mama and Daddy find out about the science quiz. Amen."*

Needless to say, my walk with God wasn't exactly ... juicy.

But it's the question so many of us have. How do we pray? What's the formula? Give me the 5-step tutorial, please, or the infographic if that's easier. Prayer can't always be simplified, but it can be simply amazing. When you meet with a good friend, you don't pull out a checklist of talk points. You just talk. What if our meditation time could be as easy as that? What if we could just hang out with God, plug into our power, shed our skin, align with our purpose, and dance with our Dreammaker?

Pray Like This

Jesus made meditation and prayer a priority in His life. He would get up early and go off by Himself and pray (Mark 1:35). Jesus knew He had a big life to live and He couldn't do it alone. He needed time with His Father. He confessed that He didn't speak on His own, but only what His Father told Him to speak (John 12:49). He also said that He didn't do anything on His own, but only what He sees His Father do (John 5:19). Jesus always said the right thing and made the right moves, but it was because He took the time to know His Father and imitate Him. And we need to do that same thing.

As moms, a lot is riding on us as well. Too many times, we speak before we get the right words, or make a move that we too often regret, and the effects can be long-lived. Gut-check time: Your life is not just about you. It's about the children who are looking up to you, the legacy you are here to build, and the generations that will come after you. Do not take this lightly. You need to get the download. You need to plug in. Fortunately, Jesus showed us how.

When His followers asked Jesus how to pray, he broke it down and made it simple. But isn't it funny how sometimes the simplest things can be the most complex? We may feel weird when we pray. We feel like it's forced or awkward or maybe just one-sided. But if you're going to take anyone's advice on how to pray, why not get it from the Big Guy, Jesus, Himself?

Jesus said, "Pray like this." He didn't say, "Use this script." He gave us a model to go by. When Jesus used the word, "like" He was telling us to get out of the formality of religion and step into the freedom of relationship. So, let's use His 10-Step Meditation Model to learn how to do this thing right!

Step One: Get Away

Jesus got up early to pray. He went off by himself. He knew how vital prayer was to fulfill His destiny, so He did what He had to do to make it happen. And I'm still perplexed on how He managed this without an alarm clock. Goals, man. Goals!

As moms, prayer needs to be a priority. Whether you sit at the kitchen table, on the toilet, or cross-legged on a meditation cushion—it doesn't matter at all. You just need to rise early enough to get time to yourself. I know that can be hard. It's usually hardest for the people who need it most. I get it. You have lots of littles who need your attention. Babies are crying, dishes are stacking up, texts are coming through. But if you think you're in high demand, just consider Jesus. People from all over were clamoring to get His attention—*"Jesus! Help my child! Jesus! Cure my leprosy! Jesus! Can I get a selfie?"* If Jesus could sneak off for some Daddy time, then so can we.

Warning: For moms, there is a strange knee-jerk reaction when the morning alarm goes off. As a survival tactic, the mom brain immediately emits the following response: "Yes, you need to meditate. Go ahead and turn off the alarm and meditate in bed. It's practically the same thing." Do NOT fall for it! "Meditating in bed" does not work. That's called dozing off. You need to make meditation intentional, purposeful, and in an upright position!

Step Two: Find Your Quiet

Meditation is not—I repeat, NOT—about "clearing your mind." It is abso-freaking-lutely impossible to get moms to think about nothing. In fact, your mind is always holding a thought. It can't *not* think about something. Meditation is not about clearing your mind. It's about focusing your thoughts.

It's hugely challenging to focus your thoughts in a noisy environment. You need quiet. If you have a noisy home, that's another reason to get up early before the troops rise up and start the attack. Grab that quiet in the morning and designate the spot. It doesn't have to be anything fancy. How you pray is more important than where you pray. So don't sweat it. Some moms have a prayer closet; others have a bathroom with a door that locks. No biggie.

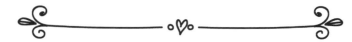

"MMU helped lead me out of a very dark hole. I was lost

in alcohol addiction and self-hatred. I felt useless, used-up, worthless, and unwanted. I had no goals or visions and everything about me and my life was a mess. My house, my marriage, our finances, but most of all, my mind was a mess! I am a totally different person today because of the amazing love of God and the guidance, teaching, coaching, continuity, and community of MMU. I am now filled with joy, contentment, and happiness. My marriage has been strengthened, we have a financial plan in place, and I have my goals set and am determined to reach them. Thank you, Hannah Keeley, for letting God use you in such a mighty way!"

—Sally B.

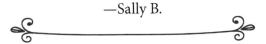

After you find a spot that is quiet and non-distracting, get comfortable. But not too comfortable. Personally, I like to wear stretchy athletic clothes (it gives me an excuse to continue my Fabletics subscription) and sit cross-legged on the floor with my butt on a cushion. But do you want secret inside information on why most people meditate in this position? I'm convinced it has nothing to do with chakras or channeling your chi. I firmly believe that this is the position that is most comfortable while being the most non-conducive to sleep. Try meditating in that easy chair without drooling, or at that kitchen table without being tempted to lay your head down for "just a minute." So, stick a pillow on the floor, plop those cute buns on it, and stay awake!

Step Three: "Our Father, Who Art in Heaven."

If you have ever meditated, one of the first instructions is to focus on your breath. But why? Why is this always the first step? I think it goes much deeper than giving you a focal point. Focusing on your breath takes you back to your original design. God created you in His image. He breathed life into you. But not just life—His life!

As you breathe in and out, remember who you are and Whose you are. As you breathe in, breathe in your creativity, your authority, your supernatural energy, your wisdom. Breathe in your very identity as God's beloved child, an heir to His throne!

As you breathe out, release. Let go of the fear, the anger, the guilt, the shame. There's no room in your life for these emotions. In fact, you were not designed to experience them. That's why your body has such adverse reactions to stress (which is just a righteous word for fear). You were not created for it. As a result, you get headaches, muscle pain, skin disorders, stomach pain, irregularity, and now I'm starting to sound like a television commercial for prescription meds! You were designed for joy—breathe it in. You were not designed for fear—breathe it out. You were designed for abundance—breathe it in. You were not designed for lack—breathe it out.

Step Four: "Hallowed be Thy Name."

Now we're gonna get a bit woo woo! Back in that meditation

class, I remember the leader talking about chakras, or energy centers in the body. There are seven different energy centers in your body from the base of your spine to the crown of your head. I'm pretty sure that was also the day that he showed us how to clear our nasal passages by flossing our nostrils. Yeah, it's a thing. For your sake, don't Google it. It's been decades and I still have that visual burned in my brain.

I wrote off the whole "chakra" thing as one more level of weirdness and went on with my life. But then something crazy happened. I was studying the names of God and learned from George Pearsons, pastor of Eagle Mountain International Church, that there were seven redemptive names of God. There's that number again—seven. I dived deeper into studying the names of God and He reminded me of Deuteronomy 28:7—" The Lord shall cause your enemies who rise up against you to be defeated before your face; they shall come out against you one way and flee before you seven ways" (AMPC).

When things come at us (and things will always come at us), it's easy to step into our emotions and get defeated. But God has a name to conquer every enemy that comes at us! When we meditate on His names, it causes our enemies to flee—seven different ways!

As a mom, I can't keep up with everything. I need devices and systems that help me manage my goals in life. Because of this, I assigned a name of God for each energy center in the body, so I could remember them easily. This way, I can just travel up my body and do a complete spiritual detox during my meditation. We're not designed to run from our enemies. We're designed to send them running!

Try it and see. It ain't no woo-woo. This is some freaking WOW-WOW!

The Tsidkenu Center: Located at the base of the spine and pelvic floor, this area is associated with your sense of safety, security, and feeling "grounded." We mistakenly think that our safety is found in our physical needs being met, but we find true security in our identity. When you know who you are, you have all you need.

"'For the time is coming,' says the Lord, 'when I will raise up a righteous descendant from King David's line. He will be a King who rules with wisdom. He will do what is just and right throughout the land. And this will be his name: The Lord Is Our Righteousness. In that day Judah will be saved and Israel will live in safety"(Jeremiah 23:5-6 NLT).

This is where we get the name Jehovah Tsidkenu, and it means, "The Lord is Our Righteousness." We dwell in safety because of who we are, not what we have. As moms, it's easy to look at our provision and lose our stability. This is when we need to get grounded in our identity as righteous. It's not something you need to become. It's who you already are. According to 2 Corinthians 5:21, Jesus became sin for us so that we could become the righteousness of God. What an amazing exchange! He takes on our sin. We take on His righteousness.

Focus on your pelvic floor area and rest your hands, palm up, on the floor beside you. With each breath, repeat the name "Tsidkenu" and imagine being grounded in righteousness. Feel the power of your true identity as His child. Rest in it. Literally. Imagine a powerful force of righteousness swirling up into you, as if you are sitting and resting in God's lap. Psalm 91:1 tells us where that "lap" is—"He who dwells in the secret place of the Most High shall abide in the shadow of the Almighty" (NKJV). You are hidden in that secret place—complete righteousness. It's who you are.

The Jireh Center: Located deep in your gut below your belly button, this area is associated with your creativity and emotional identity. Moms often struggle with a feeling of lack. We have limiting beliefs that keep us from being and experiencing everything God has for us in life. We hold back. We play small. And you can't create anything out of lack. But when you know you have access to "everything we need according to His riches in glory in Christ Jesus" (Philippians 4:19), and that He "delights in your prosperity" (Psalm 35:27), and that "every good and perfect gift comes from the Father" (James 1:17), then you can understand that because God is unlimited, so is your provision.

"Then Abraham looked up and saw a ram caught by its horns in a thicket. So he took the ram and sacrificed it as a burnt offering in place of his son. Abraham named the place Yahweh-Yireh (which means 'the Lord will provide') ..." (Genesis 22:13-14 NLT).

The name, "Jehovah Jireh" means the Lord will provide. But I need you to see something here. The ram was on its way to the thicket before the need even presented itself. Whatever you need to fulfill your destiny is already on its way to you.

Focus on your lower region, below your belly button, while you rest your hands, one on top of the other, palm up, in your lap. With each breath, repeat the name "Jireh" as you see provision pouring into your life out of God's rich storehouse. He is not lacking. Therefore, neither are you. See His riches and goodness pouring into you and overflowing out of you, filling in every gap, every space, until it pushes out all feelings of lack.

"God is so good! My 90-Day Challenge inside MMU has been on money and wealth. The tithing teaching really tugged at my heart. We started tithing two weeks ago. Well, yesterday my husband came home from work. He had gotten a bonus at work and I also got a settlement check from a law suit."

—Danielle P.

One key method to learn to trust His future provision is to go back and remember His past provision. Remember three different moments in your life when you were filled with gratitude. They don't have to be big moments to make a big impact. Step into those moments as if you are experiencing them all over again. See what you saw. Hear what you heard. Feel what you felt. Let this gratitude swell up inside you.

As you meditate in gratitude, you can rest in His provision. You don't have to worry about how it's going to happen. The ingredients are already there, and God has the perfect recipe. If you ever feel hopeless, you're just looking in the wrong direction. Look to Jesus, the Author and Finisher of your faith. What He began in you will be completed. It's already on its way. See it. Feel it. Receive it.

The Shammah Center: Located in the center of your body, right above your navel, this is your core. But guess what is actually your "core?" You got it—God Almighty! Many moms experience poor self-esteem, confusion, or lack of confidence because they forget who and Whose they really are! Fear is often manifested in the belly. Ever felt "butterflies in your stomach?" But as a child of God, fear has no place in your life. It is empowering to be in the presence of God. But what is even more empowering is knowing the presence of God is within you.

According to Acts 1:8, "you will receive power when the Holy Spirit comes upon you." Jesus explained that it was good that He was going to His Father because He would send back the Holy Spirit to dwell within us. And He did. On the day of Pentecost, the Holy Spirit came down like a windstorm and settled like fire among and within God's people. You, my sweet friend, are the temple of the Holy Spirit. God looked all over for the perfect place to dwell, and He picked YOU! Not because you were perfect, but because He loves you. Love makes a house a home!

"And from that day the name of the city will be 'The Lord is There.'" *(Ezekiel 48:35 NLT).*

The name Jehovah Shammah means "The Lord is There." And He is, right there inside you. Jesus explains it like this, 'You will realize that I am in my Father, and you are in me, and I am in you" (John 14:20). We're all in this together! I Corinthians 3:16 asks, "Do you not know that you are the temple of God and that the Spirit of God dwells in you?" (NKJV). The root cause of any fear that creeps in your life is not the storms you face, but forgetting that with God inside, you are waterproof!

Place one hand over the other and rest them against the center of your body, below your chest and above your navel. Repeat the name "Shammah" as you feel the presence of God within you. Imagine fire in your belly, first a small flame, then with each breath growing bigger and more powerful, until it spreads throughout your entire body. Like the wind at Pentecost, your breath feeds the fire within you. Imagine the power of God filling you with fire, radiance, and light. No fear can exist in the presence of God. And that presence is within you!

The Ra-ah Center: Located at your heart, right there in your chest, this is the area associated with compassion and love. Ever felt your chest tighten up when you got stressed out? Stress is just a white-washed term for fear. And "… perfect love drives out fear …" (I John 4:18 NIV).

With motherhood comes overwhelm. We all feel it at some point (which is probably what led you to get this book in the first place). Stress makes us lose hope and puts a strain on our relationships. Stress happens when we depend on our abilities and resources instead of God's. Without Him, you're nothing. But with Him, you're everything! You, plus God, is always a majority. If Jesus didn't think He could do anything apart from God, what makes you think you can? He even said, "By Myself I can do nothing ..." (John 5:30 NIV). You need God. And good news—you got Him!

"The Lord is my shepherd; I shall not want. He makes me to lie down in green pastures; he leads me beside the still waters. He restores my soul; He leads me in the paths of righteousness for His name's sake" (Psalm 23:1-3 (NKJV)

The name Jehovah Ra-ah means "The Lord my Shepherd." There will always be an opportunity for you to feel stressed out and overwhelmed. But every time you find yourself in that place, you can trace it back to pulling away from God's power and wisdom and depending upon your own. You're a sheep. And, let's just get real. Sometimes sheep can be stupid. They eat garbage. They'll get stuck in shrubs. Once, when we were driving down a road in Iceland, we saw a sheep just jogging along, all by himself, right in the middle of the road. Lost as can be, and blithely content to stay that way. You can be sure I put it on Instagram!

Place your hands over your heart and just feel it beating. Lift up gratitude for your heart, your body, and the love that pours in and through you. Repeat the name "Ra-ah" with each breath as you let go of your concerns and trust in God's care. In 1 Peter 5:7 we are told to "cast all your cares upon Him for He cares for you." He is your Good Shepherd. He is your Caretaker. He'll take the cares, but He won't snatch them out of your grasp. You need to let them go. With each breath, feel the lightness of releasing those cares. One by one, let them go. He can handle them way better than you can. Focus on the love of God, and let that love swell up in your heart and fill you up. When you know how much He loves you, you can trust Him and let go.

The Rapha Center: Located at your throat, this is the perfect place where we communicate—both with the world and with ourselves. You may have areas in your life where you need healing, both physical and emotional. Healing begins with communication. What are you saying about your emotional symptoms—the guilt, the bitterness, the shame, the heartbreak? What are you saying about your physical symptoms—the headaches, the disease, the weight, the blood pressure? Because your words create your world.

"He said, If you will listen carefully to the voice of the Lord your God and do what is right in his sight, obeying his commands and keeping all his decrees, then I will not make you suffer any of the diseases I sent on the Egyptians; for I am the Lord who heals you" *Exodus 15:26 (NLT).*

The name Jehovah Rapha, means "The Lord Who Heals." Healing is included in the covenant we have with God through Jesus. And, personally, I want every bit of what Jesus died to give me.

The other day I bought a new bottle of foundation makeup. As I was getting ready to grab my bag and leave the store, the saleswoman stopped me and asked, "Don't you want your bag of goodies?" Evidently, my brand of makeup was offering a promotion so that if I buy foundation, I get a glittery gold bag full of lipstick, mascara, eyeliner, highlighting powder, and a perfume sample absolutely free. You know I grabbed that bad boy before I left the store!

That's the problem a lot of moms have with their faith. They believe Jesus will give them eternal life in heaven, but they stop there. Jesus wasn't crucified just so we could go to heaven after we die. He was crucified to bring heaven to earth while we're still alive. I got the foundation, but I want the goodies, too! He promises us an abundant life, and, yes, healing is included in that. And how you're feeling always goes back to what you're saying. Proverbs 12:18 tell us, "the tongue of the wise brings healing." So, speak up!

"When I started Mom Mastery University, I was at a point in life where I had no vision and I was perishing inside. I didn't care about where we were headed and had no energy or strength to kickstart it. I needed help! I found MMU and started to see the light, the fogginess started to clear, and my heart and eyes were beginning to open. I found my zing and things started to look up. I was starting to live a life that I had dreamt of but didn't know how to attain. People around me

started to see a change and liked what they saw. This is just the beginning. It feels so good to be taking one step at a time, becoming a better me."

—Bernice E.

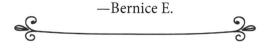

Place your hands gently over the base of your throat where your collarbones meet. Repeat the name "Rapha" with each breath as you imagine healing power pouring in and through your body. See any areas of pain, including emotional pain such as strained relationships, as red. With each breath, imagine white light, God's healing power, penetrating those areas and swirling throughout your body. Instead of wanting to be healed, see yourself as healed already. It's not something you are striving for, it's your current state, and you are training your body to fall in line with the reality that already exists.

The Shalom Center: Located on your forehead, this area represents your vision, intuition, and understanding. We know the word, "shalom" to mean "peace," but it actually means a whole lot more. The Hebrew word shalom means a state of completeness or wholeness, where nothing is lacking, nothing is broken, and nothing is missing. That's the kind of peace God wants to give His children. According to Philippians 4:7, it's a peace that passes all understanding that guards your heart and mind. Ever found that when things appear broken or out of place in your life you get headaches? Yep, you nailed it!

"And Gideon built an altar to the Lord there and named it

Yahweh-Shalom (which means 'the Lord is peace')" (Judges 6:24 NLT)

Just before building this altar, Gideon had been shooting the breeze with someone and was unaware it was an angel he was talking to, face to face. Immediately after realizing who it was, he was shocked. He was afraid that the power of being in the presence of an angel of God would kill him. He then heard the voice of God say to him, "Peace! Do not be afraid. You are not going to die."

The most difficult reality to face is not our limitations, but the truth that we have no limitations. If you are looking at your future through the lens of your humanity, you will constantly fall into confusion, wanting to pull back and play small. But if you can switch lenses for a moment and look at your life as an expression of God through you, suddenly you become unlimited. Colossians 1:27 refers to this switch as a "mystery." Wholeness is no longer something you strive to attain. It is Christ in you, the hope of glory. Your brilliance is almost too much to bear, and like Gideon, you want to run and hide from it. No more, Mama. Face the wonder of who you really are.

Place your hands gently on your forehead and repeat the name "Shalom" with every breath. As you do, imagine the peace of God, like a beautiful, iridescent, sparkling liquid, pouring into you, filling every gap. Leaving nothing broken, nothing missing. Filling your "natural" with His "super" until you become what He designed you to be in the first place—supernatural.

The Nissi Center: Located at the top of your head, the crown, this area is associated with inspiration and connectivity to God. Unfortunately, this is the area that most busy moms tend to neglect. When you've got laundry to fold, calls to make, a doctor's appointment to keep, and a diaper that is so urine-logged it's about to drop off your baby's bottom, you're not feeling that inspired. And when you're not filled with inspiration, you're often weighed down with desperation.

Desperate Housewives isn't just a reality show. It quickly becomes our identity if we don't become intentional with our spirituality. And desperation leads to feelings of failure. If we're not careful, we're back to Mom Fatigue Syndrome. With God there is no failure, just more opportunities.

"... After the victory, the Lord instructed Moses, 'Write this down on a scroll as a permanent reminder, and read it aloud to Joshua: I will erase the memory of Amalek from under heaven.' Moses built an altar there and named it Yahweh-Nissi (which means 'the Lord is my Banner')" (Exodus 17:14-15 NLT).

Joshua was getting ready to become the leader of the Israelites, replacing Moses. He had big shoes to fill and new places to go, places he had never been. God knew He had to create a way to remind Joshua that he wasn't going in alone. God was going before him and behind him, and was a protective banner over him.

Oh, the places you will go, Mama! New levels to reach, new roles to fill, and new victories to accomplish. Your connection to God isn't just helpful, it is imperative. In Song of Solomon 2:4, you find that His banner over you is love. When you know that His impenetrable love is all around you, you can move forward with boldness and confidence. Let your battle cry be that of Psalm 33:22—"Let your unfailing love surround us, Lord, for our hope is in you alone" (NLT). God doesn't give you hope; He is your hope. There is a reason this area is at the top of your head—He is your crowning glory!

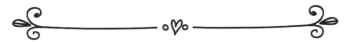

"I was battling depression, struggled emotionally with the thoughts of abandoning my 5 kids because I thought they would be better off without me, and on the verge of going back on medication when I started Mom Mastery University. I am so excited to share that God has healed my emotions and my marriage over the past 90 days. I'm stronger today! I have overcome depression without going back on medication. I am enjoying my kids, my husband, and my life! My whole family is thankful for Hannah Keeley and MMU because I'm a better mom/wife/woman today than I have been in a very long time!"
—Lori B.

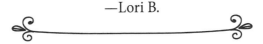

Lift your hands up and repeat the name "Nissi" with each breath. See that love of God surrounding you—above you, beneath you, around you. Imagine it like a glorious cloud of light swirling around you in the center. Then let it pour through the top of your head, swirling around in your body. Then let this love surge within you and pour out of you, into the lives of others—your children, your family, your friends, your clients, your business partners, your team members, and your support group. Send these people the same love that God so freely offers you.

Step Five: "Thy Kingdom Come, Thy Will Be Done on Earth as It Is in Heaven."

God's kingdom is no longer something we must wait on. It has already come! When Jesus was explaining God's kingdom, He said, "… The kingdom of God does not come with observation; nor will they say, 'See here!' or 'See there!' For indeed, the kingdom of God is within you" (Luke 17:20-21 NKJV). You don't have to see it to know it exists. It is within you, existing in the spiritual realm, waiting for you to add the belief and the action to bring it into the physical. And we do it by faith.

As children of God we have the right to call the end from the beginning. God breathed His creative power into us, but it is up to us to put it into operation. God has given you a vision for your life. You don't have to wonder if it's His will. God's will is not a mystery. His Word is His will. And when you know His promises in His Word, you can create them in your world.

God does not call us to endure life on earth until we finally get VIP treatment in heaven. He calls us to bring the heavenly experience to earth. This is the step where you visualize those goals and dreams God has given you. Imagine your top five goals (your "Fab 5"). As you go through each one, put yourself into the goal. Imagine it on every sensory level as if you are experiencing it right now. Your subconscious (inner mom) cannot tell the difference between real and imaginary, so give her something to work with!

Step Six: "Give Us This Day Our Daily Bread."

Have you ever started preparing something in the kitchen and then realized you were missing some ingredients? Many moms embark on their days without rehearsing how they should go. When you do this, you are missing the necessary ingredients to create what you desire. Whether you are making bread, writing a screenplay, training for a competition, or creating a day, you need to begin with the end in mind. That is why you should always meditate in the morning. You need to script your day from the beginning.

During this step, imagine you going throughout your day. See the work done and your MAP completed. Don't just see what you're doing, but imagine how you're doing it—with joy, excitement, and positive energy. You can even imagine typical scenarios that create stress in your life, and see yourself handling them like a pro. It's your life, and you call the shots, so see the day played out in your mind.

Step Seven: "Forgive Us Our Trespasses as We Forgive Those Who Trespass Against Us."

The biggest thing that can stand between you and the life you want to create is holding onto offense. All of God's promises rest on the law of love. If we are not operating in love, we can't rest in His promises. We can have all the faith in the world, but without love, it is useless. It's like having 10 tons of dynamite, but no match. The power is there, but you need love to release it and let it go to work.

"Hannah, I have to tell you … when you prayed to renounce bitterness and unforgiveness in a marriage, God freed me in a way that was such a total 'about face.' I can't even fully describe it. I asked my husband for forgiveness that night for being so bitter and angry toward him. Our marriage was falling apart. Now we have hope. Thank you for allowing God to use you. You have no idea."

—Kate W.

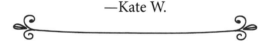

Matthew 5:23-24 tells us, "So if you are presenting a sacrifice at the altar in the Temple and you suddenly remember that someone has something against you, leave your sacrifice there at the altar. Go and be reconciled to that person. Then come and offer your sacrifice to God" (NLT). Our morning meditation is a sacrifice, but living in love always takes precedence. If you are holding bitterness or unforgiveness toward people in your life, this is the time when you release it. This isn't a suggestion. It is a command. Colossians 3:13 reminds us to "… forgive anyone

who offends you. Remember, the Lord forgave you, so you must forgive others" (NLT). God never tells us to do what is impossible with His help. Forgiveness doesn't absolve what that person did. It releases you from being in bondage because of it. Forgive, and let the love flow.

Step Eight: "Lead Us Not Into Temptation but Deliver Us from Evil."

I Corinthians 10:13 tells us that "The temptations in your life are no different from what others experience. And God is faithful. He will not allow the temptation to be more than you can stand. When you are tempted, he will show you a way out so that you can endure" (NLT). Have you ever noticed that you always give in to temptation when you feel weak and defeated? Satan's busiest time of day is late afternoon. He's striking down moms left and right!

Weakness results when you step out of a place of power. And we do that when we feel less than who we are. During this step, build yourself up in who you are! If you are holding anything against yourself, now is when you let it go. Shame and guilt will defeat you at every turn if you let them. Don't even give them a place in your life. God has forgiven you, now you must forgive yourself. Let it go. That's not you anymore. Paul said, "I don't look back." He knew if he looked back at his life as a murderer, he couldn't make progress toward his calling as an apostle. God has called you for big things, Mama. Forgive yourself and move on.

Step Nine: "Thine Is the Kingdom, the Power, and the Glory, Forever."

Wrap up your meditation by stepping into your rightful position as a daughter of the Most High God. Luke 17:21 says the kingdom of God is within you! Luke 10:19 says we have power over the enemy! Romans 8:17 says we share in His glory! He died so we could live. And not just to stay alive, but to really LIVE!

Take several deep, cleansing breaths. With each one, feel that power growing stronger and stronger. When your tank is full, open your eyes and get ready to rock your world.

Step Ten: The Three Questions

As you move forward, it's a great idea to keep track of where you've been. Wrap up your meditation by taking a moment to journal your answers to these three questions:

What do I need to release to God today?
What am I grateful for today? Why?
What am I hearing from God today?

Now you're powered up and ready, Mama. Go forth and conquer!

Go to www.hannahkeeley.com/meditation
to download your free meditation audio

STEP EIGHT: MANIFESTATION

Chapter 17: Got Your Goal Mates?

I'm pretty sure every girl goes through a stage in life where she wants to be in the spotlight—either on stage or on camera. She gets bitten by the Hollywood bug and wants to be the next Disney star. I have two sets of girls—two at the head, and two at the rear. There's a 10-year age difference between them, during which I gave birth to three boys. Both sets were bitten—and bitten hard!

With my oldest daughters, I wanted to scratch that itch so I found the cheapest opportunity I could. A flier posted at our grocery store announced auditions for Annie at a local children's theater. I had never heard of the theater but decided to take my chances. The auditions consisted of children singing "Happy Birthday" to a couple of ladies sitting in the theater. I say "theater" loosely because it was an old warehouse shed with cement floors and metal walls. Ten girls auditioned, and not surprisingly, they all made the cut and got roles in the play.

It was one heck of a production. I believe they rehearsed for about two weeks. The girls stumbled across their lines and giggled through most of it. The director coerced a friend of hers to play the role of Daddy Warbucks, which he did with the help of index cards. I'm also pretty sure no man alive has ever had worse body odor. You could smell him from the back of the theater, which was the fifth row.

My daughter got the enviable role of Annie, which meant she had to struggle to hold on to the collar of Sandy while singing *Tomorrow* from a wooden platform supported by cinder blocks. As she hit the crescendo, Sandy twisted out of her grasp and let loose through the warehouse, umm, theater. She went up and down all five rows, jumping on the parents in the audience and sniffing around until she found a discarded Chick-fil-A wrapper in the corner and ran out the back with it in her mouth. And I'm sure, from the looks of Sandy as she hightailed it out of the theater that she was grossly miscast. Sandy was a boy. Nay, a man.

A month after the show closed, we drove by the warehouse, umm, theater, and saw a "condemned" sign on the front door.

Looking back, my daughters have frequently inquired about this strange theater experience. They are sure I dropped them off at the local crack house when I needed a break, and are still wondering if they were being used as an experiment in money laundering. Needless to say, it wasn't the best experience, although we have gotten plenty of laughs out of it.

Now fast forward 10 years.

My second pair of daughters also got bitten by the bug. Since the crack house was condemned, and especially because I didn't want to repeat the process, I found the best children's theater in the area. It was quite a financial investment, but I wanted to do it right. This theater did not mess around. They held auditions and classes for kids, and for the first several auditions, my daughters didn't make the plays. And these plays they put on—oh my goodness! They could rival any Broadway production!

I decided to invest in private training for my daughters' auditions. Once they received this, they were able to land roles in the ensemble for the next play. They had to sign a contract that they would not miss any rehearsals. The theater group hired professional set builders, makeup artists, lighting and sound professionals, directors, and choreographers. Rehearsals were demanding and exhausting. They lasted for months and would go for entire days. My daughters went from complete novices in theater to learning how to block scenes, harmonize, get in character, and act like professionals.

The actors in the theater group take it very seriously. Many have graduated and gone into professional theater. It was so funny to see them at practice. During a break, they would stop and act like kids—playing ball, folding cootie catchers, chasing each other, and acting goofy. Then when it was time to rehearse, they magically transformed into little, responsible, talented adults—listening, working, following directions. After learning and growing in this type of setting, my daughters went on to snag roles in several commercials and professional productions.

It was quite a contrast from the crack house.

You Can't Break This Law

There is a law at work, and you can see it in my daughters' theater.

It's called the Law of Association. Basically, we become like the people we spend the most time with. My older daughters learned nothing in their theater experience, except how to tell the difference between a male and female dog. However, with my younger daughters, they learned vast amounts of information and rose to a level of professionalism that truly surprised me. They had potential locked away inside and it took being surrounded by excellence to bring it out.

This is the last step—Manifestation. The entire method will do you no good unless you know how to continue the process to Manifestation. It requires three things—community, coaching, and continuity. The best way to keep up the process is to surround yourself with excellence, and put it on repeat.

"As a teen, I struggled with depression. I attempted to end my life at the age of 15. The pain and guilt of past mistakes and abuse left me broken. As a wife and mother of five children, living in a new state with my in-laws, I felt desperate, unworthy, and unqualified. I had horrible migraines. I was sure my husband and kids would be better off without me. I wanted to die. It's hard to even write this. I left many nights in my car and would drive and drive, contemplating crashing the car to end my life. But God had another plan. One day He led me to a video of Hannah. I found HOPE and began my healing journey. At Mom Mastery Live, I experienced unbelievable breakthrough and total healing from the bondage of

past hurts. And no more migraines!"
—Nettie R.

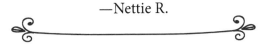

Abraham understood this, only because God demanded it of him.

"Now [in Haran] the Lord said to Abram, Go for yourself [for your own advantage] away from your country, from your relatives and your father's house, to the land that I will show you. And I will make of you a great nation, and I will bless you [with abundant increase of favors] and make your name famous and distinguished, and you will be a blessing [dispensing good to others]" (Genesis 12:1-2 AMPC).

God knew that if He was going to get Abraham to rise up in his potential and carry out the promise placed on his life, He was going to have to get him out of Haran. He was surrounded by idol worshippers—in his family, his community, everywhere. God needed a man who was going to stand out and make a difference, and it couldn't happen in his hometown.

The Law of Association works every single time. You can't break it. You can only use it. Most people use it to their disadvantage. They are surrounded by small thinkers, so they shrink their beliefs to fit the company they keep. Use this law in your favor! Just like God did with Abraham, He is lifting you up and out of your comfort zone. He is promoting you to a level of excellence and abundance, and that means leaving the small thinkers behind. You know what they say—if you're the smartest person in the room, you're in the wrong room. You're in the big leagues now, Mama! You need people who will support you, encourage you, inspire you, and lead you to greatness. You need goal mates!

Who's Making the Cut?

Abraham obeyed God—kinda. He told him to leave his relatives, but he brought along his nephew, Lot. This ended up being a hindrance to him. They eventually had to separate; and it was painful. It stalled his progress and he even had to risk his life and his entire army to go save Lot's butt. Eventually, Lot ended up drunk in a cave with a pillar of salt for a wife. You just can't change some people, no matter what you do.

Whether you like it or not, the Law of Association is at work in your life. This area is particularly problematic for moms because we don't always form relationships intentionally. We form them out of convenience. Our friends become the people we go to church with, the moms in our playgroups, or the people hanging out at the dance studio or soccer field.

Jim Rohn, author, entrepreneur and motivational speaker extraordinaire, said, "You are the average of the five people you spend the most time with." That quote is often tossed around at business conferences and motivational meet-ups as an incentive to grow yourself personally by putting the Law of Association to work for you. But where does that leave moms? The people we spend the most time with are often just learning how to poop in the toilet or struggling to dress themselves. Is that our fate?

As moms, we need to create a core community for ourselves that enriches and inspires us, but where you do we find these people? It's not like we can go off to conferences and join masterminds. We're trying to get dinner on the table! Stick with me. I've got answers for you.

When God tells us to separate, He's serious. He knows the power of the Law of Association. That's why He often pushes us to move out from where we are, and the people we're with. Whether we like it or not, the people we hang out with will either make us or break us. And if you don't want to live their lives, don't take their advice.

"Walk with the wise and become wise, for a companion of fools suffers harm" (Proverbs 13:20 NIV).

How do you tell if you are a companion of fools? Sit back and imagine your social circles. See yourself at the social gatherings, the classes, the group meetings. Are you surrounded by people who—

Groan about their health?
Grumble about their finances?
Gripe about politics, the weather, or the latest bug that's going around?

"I used to be depressed and negative. I have always been very friendly and try to smile to everyone, but inside I would have a deep sadness and insecurities. I remember asking God one day in tears if I could ever feel happiness. His answer was and is 'Yes and Amen!' I have learned so much from Hannah and from all of the mamas that I could write pages and pages! Every time I think how I got to MMU I feel so grateful. I know it was God's hand that brought me here."

—Rozanna H.

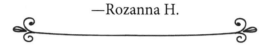

You already know if the answer is "yes" or not. And if you're a mom, I'm guessing it's an affirmative. We can't be as selective about our companions because we are stuck with them out of necessity. We can't always choose our companions; sometimes they are selected for us because of our obligations as moms. We're stuck in the waiting room at the dance studio and we can't choose which butts fill the other seats.

Eleanor Roosevelt once said, "Great minds discuss ideas; average minds discuss events; small minds discuss people." So, what do you do when God is transforming you to live a big life, but you're surrounded by small minds? Here are four ways to switch things up …

#1—Make time for it. The first knee-jerk reaction for most moms when it comes to socialization is, "Ain't nobody got time for that."

But if your fate is determined by your companions, you better make time for that! One way to foster a healthy core community is to lessen the time you spend with people who weigh you down and increase the time you spend with people who lift you up. Who do you know who always believes in you and encourages you? Who do you know who refuses to tolerate any of your belly-achin'? Those are the people you need to hang out with.

#2—Pray for it. God wants you to walk with the wise; but how can you fly like an eagle if you're surrounded by chickens? Easy. Claim His Word over the situation. If He commands you to walk with the wise, then ask Him to bring the wise to you. But don't beg. The prayers of a righteous man (or mom) avail much, not the prayers of a desperate one (James 5:16). Just pray, "God, Your word says to walk with the wise. I'm asking You right now to bring those wise people to me, or bring me to them. Surround me with them. Thank You that they are coming into my life, right now." Then every day, thank Him that they are on the way. You may even want to add an affirmation to your audio recording—"I attract the wisest people into my life and they inspire and instruct me to reach new levels of abundance."

#3—Make it intentional. As moms, we can't always choose our company, but we can become intentional about choosing our companions. Seek out people who are living the life you want to live, with the finances you want, the marriage you seek, and the lifestyle you are building. Wanna know a secret? The entire reason I started my podcast was so that I had a method by which to make connections with successful people. Experts and authors were much more willing to be "interviewed" than, "Could you spend 30 minutes with me so I can pick your brain on how you reached your level of success?" One podcaster who is a multi-millionaire was asked the question, "If all you had was $1,000 and you had to start over, what would you do?" He replied that he would spend all the money on taking the most successful people he could find out to dinner. Now, that's intentional!

#4—Go digital. We live in such an amazing age! We truly have access to the most successful people in the world at the touch of a button. I soak in the tub with Creflo Dollar. I share the treadmill with Tony Robbins. I drive Joyce Meyer around in my car. I do my chores with Zig Ziglar in my back pocket. I lounge by the pool with Oprah Winfrey. You can seek out the wisest companions in the world by listening to audiobooks and podcasts. I listen to a minimum of one hour of teaching daily. If you think that's excessive, then get a bigger picture for your life. God is leading you to a promised land; why not listen to the people who already found the way there?

Tough News You Don't Want to Hear

God tells us to rejoice with those who rejoice and weep with those who weep (Romans 12:15). Initially, you would think it's easier to rejoice. But when it comes to your friend circle, you may find the exact opposite. It's much easier to share someone's trouble than it is to share someone's success. This is one way to know if your friends make the cut or not—do they truly celebrate your success and encourage you along that path? Or does your success intimidate them?

Many of your current companions are not going to be comfortable with you rising to new levels of abundance in your life. They will want that woman back who grumbled about being exhausted and overwhelmed all the time. Why? Because your failure makes their failure feel so much better, and, conversely, your success makes their failure hurt so much worse. It's not their fault; they are not truly wishing ill will upon you. It's just human nature to want to feel comfortable and secure.

"I just want to post a testimony of Mom Mastery University and the skills it has equipped me with! I just finished my Bachelor of Science in Nursing, while parenting and home-schooling 4 kids and my home wasn't a total bomb all the time. Most of all I was able to stay focused on Him for my strength! God will provide a way for all of us to do what He has called us to!"

—Eva P.

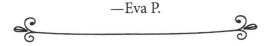

You will find as you continue with the Mom Mastery Method, that you will rise to new levels of abundance. Many of your friends won't be too fond of that. Your success turns a mirror on their lives and forces them to come to grips with a reality they may not be willing to face. That's why when you start exercising and losing weight, your friend will surprise you by taking you out to TGI Fridays for their Tennessee Whiskey Cake. It's not that she wants you to get fat; she just feels much better about herself when you are.

Keep loving your friends, just loosen your grip on the ones that are not a positive influence and be ready to move on.

The Power of a Coach

You're growing your team. Now it's time to get your coach. The first time I ever invested in a coach, was with a woman who had built her company to seven figures and was willing to help me do the same. When she told me how much it would cost to hire her as a coach, she informed me "nine ninety-seven a month." In my naïve state, I assumed she meant $9.97 a month. I was like, "That's all? Sure!" Then she sent me the bill—$997.00 a month!

When I picked my jaw up off the ground, I had a choice to make—look like an idiot, back out of the deal, and stay where I was; or do the hard thing, find a way to pay that money and grow to new levels.

I did the hard thing.

To this day, I can't recall how I was able to scrounge up that much money every month. Sometimes I was a few days late, but the money always came through—eventually. After six months of her coaching, I launched a program that brought in $17,000. Was it worth it? Absolutely. I don't even want to think about where

I would be today if I had not taken that huge, heart-pounding, gut-wrenching leap of faith.

Good coaches are worth their weight in gold. They can help you avoid the mistakes. They can show you the shortcuts. They can give you the formulas. Today, I'm able to coach moms only because of the coaches I have had over the years. It started with "nine ninety-seven." Today, I invest at least 10 percent of my income into coaching and training.

Don't try to do this alone. Manifesting your dreams can't happen in isolation. You need a team, and you need a coach.

You're worth it.

You always have been.

You always will be.

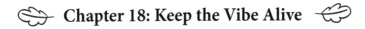

Chapter 18: Keep the Vibe Alive

I had no idea when I woke up that morning that I would be trapped when I went to bed. I was in Dallas at a conference and planned to fly out the next morning. My husband, Blair, called and told me a cold front was coming through Virginia that night, but I wasn't concerned. After all, it was sunny and warm where I was. Who cares about a little cold front?

As I was packing my suitcase that evening for my flight the next morning, I got a text from the airline telling me my flight had changed and I had to call the airline as soon as possible. I didn't think much about it. I've had plenty of delayed flights before. However, when I called, I didn't expect to hear that my flight had been canceled. Not delayed, not rerouted—canceled. My heart started beating a little faster. I had to get home. My little girl was having a birthday, and I'm her mom! I can only be away from my babies for a short amount of time before I spontaneously combust!

I spoke with a woman at the airline and told her I needed to get home. She told me there were no planes flying in to Richmond, Virginia. Like, nothing. It was impossible. They had closed the airport.

Whoa. Did she just use the word, "impossible?"

"Well, how close can you get me?" I asked.

"All other flights going anywhere near Richmond are booked solid," she replied.

"There's got to be something," I said. "Could you look again?" She begrudgingly obliged.

"I don't think it's going to do you much good, but I'll check."

I waited on the other end of the line, hearing her type on the keyboard and praying for something to open up.

"Oh my goodness!" she exclaimed. "A seat just opened up on a flight going into Charlottesville, Virginia. You're going to have some layovers in a couple of other cities, but you'll be able to get there by tomorrow night."

"I'll take it—please!" I yelled into the phone. I had no idea where Charlottesville was.

She got me set up with my flight; and I immediately called my husband to share the good news (or so I thought). I called him and told him. He was silent.

"What's wrong?" I asked. "I thought you'd be happy."

"It's not that I'm not happy," he replied. "It's just that I'm not sure you'll be able to get home. There's no way I can get out, and nothing's coming in. Hannah, I don't think you realize what it's like here. This is the heaviest snow we've had in over four years.

There's already three feet of snow outside and they can't even get inside the area to scrape the roads. I literally am snowbound. And Charlottesville is over 60 miles away. I think you're going to have to cancel that and just stay until they can open the airport back up."

I would not be deterred. I had found a way to get close. And close was all I needed. I would get home. This mama bear wasn't going to stop until she reached her cave.

"Then I'll catch a cab and go as far as possible and walk the rest of the way," I said.

"Hannah," he said. "Be sensible. You can't walk. You'll have suitcases with you and at least five miles of road that haven't been scraped."

"I'm coming home," I said, adamantly. "If I have to steal two tennis rackets, strap them to my feet, and Sasquatch it all the way with luggage tied to my back, I'm coming home."

Blair knew it was pointless to argue with me at that point. It was the point of no return. I was determined, and you don't mess with a mom on a mission!

I flew out that morning. After several layovers in cities I can't even recall, I arrived that evening to a tiny airport in Charlottesville. When I stepped off the plane, I honestly didn't know what I was in for, but I was ready for the battle. When I got to baggage claim, I saw Blair standing there, waiting for me. I burst into tears and ran into his arms. I was ready to walk five miles in the snow to get home to my family, but there he was, with open arms and a huge smile, and an aching back.

"My purpose didn't come to life until I discovered my passion and was intentional with my daily living. Vision, direction, and FOCUS are HUGE factors missing in today's busy world. Because of MMU I now know my purpose and live in passion!"

—Jessica H.

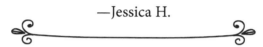

I found out later that he had dug his way out of the neighborhood, literally. It took him eight and a half hours of digging a path for his car to get out of the snow and onto the roads that had been cleared. He had woken up at 6am that morning and started digging while it was still dark outside. Almost 11 hours later, he was waiting for me at the Charlottesville airport.

Something happens when a mom is on a mission. It's almost like heaven and earth bend to her will. She is a powerful force to be reckoned with, so get out of her way. And she is not alone in the struggle. Her faithful God is on the other side of that mountain, moving it out of the way.

God is ready to come to your aid, but you must be willing to keep fighting.

Quitting Time Is Over

If you were going to quit, you should have done it before making it to the last chapter. If you wanted to stay exhausted and over-whelmed, you never should have even read the first page. Now you're in it. Now you're responsible. You're holding the keys. Whether you drive or not is up to you.

It's no longer time to quit. That hour has passed. It's go time. Wake up

And that's all you have to do—just go. You don't have to get it perfect. You just have to get it going. You've got the method, now you just need to stay the course. It's time to win—at life, at home, with your body, with your finances, and in your family. You've given yourself permission to fail long enough. Why not do some-thing totally crazy and give yourself permission to succeed? God already laid the framework; you just need to rise up and walk it out.

"In January we went from having nothing left at the end of the month to saving about $290 in one month! The Mom Mastery Method has changed my life from the inside-out. Praising God for His goodness. He gets all the glory!"

—Lindsay D.

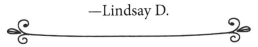

Something happens when a mom makes a choice. Not a fickle

little decision on a whim, but a clear, no-turning-back, conscious choice. When you make that choice, you just start moving, and you keep moving. You let nothing pull you away from your target. It's like the universe knows who it can mess with and who it can work with. And when the universe sees that mom coming with her fists clenched and that "take no prisoners" look in her eyes, it just knows—give her whatever she needs.

God has already made the way. Jesus finished the work on the cross. The stage is set for your production. You don't have to have it all figured out. You don't need to know where that foot is going to fall when you take the next step. All you have to do is take it. It's funny: When we decide we're going to go the distance, no matter what, that's when God intercedes and shortens the path.

Get fierce! If you have to Sasquatch it all the way to your Promised Land, be ready to do it, and don't give up. The distance between the dream and the Manifestation is discipline. Every. Single. Day.

The Three-Legged Stool

We have an old milking stool that I keep in my office to remind me of the three legs of Manifestation—community, coaching, and continuity. You already know the importance of community. Every day, I invest in the women inside Mom Mastery University, reaching out, building up, and praying over them. That's my community. We encourage each other. If I'm getting threatened in a dark alley, those are the women I want to have my back. We fiercely protect each other. Yes, they will cut you. Watch out.

You also understand how important it is to have a coach. I plug into teaching every single day, whether digitally or on a video call with one of my mentors. My parents taught me when I was little to learn something new every day. I try to learn as much as possible and execute what I learn. It's dangerous to get in "sponge mode." We spend so much time reading, listening, and learning, but fail to execute. A sponge was made to get results. You're not going to get results in your life unless you squeeze some of that learning out in execution. Knowledge without execution is pointless. Learn and do, or don't even learn at all.

"I am incredibly grateful for all Mom Mastery University has done for my life. I am a full-time working mom. My husband works out of town a lot and we have no support nearby. I was in tears multiple times per day because doing it all alone was too hard. MMU has taught me to not do it all alone. I am truly happy for the first time in three years! I am able to be present when doing activities because I am not worrying about al the things that need to be done! I am excited to share this with other moms. I want all of them to see how enjoyable life can be!"

—Tricia S.

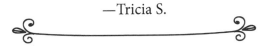

But guess what? You already learned. It's too late to turn back now. It's time to execute! And that's the third leg of Manifestation—continuity. You have to want it so badly that you show up and keep showing up. If there's no way, you find a way. Make reaching your goals a question of "when" not "if," because if you keep your vision alive, keep speaking your affirmations, keep writing your goals, and keep doing your routines daily, it's just a matter of time. You will reach them. No question.

Violent Moms

The truth about your success is that you are already successful. You are already rich. You are already abundant. You are already loving, kind, brilliant, and massively productive. You just have to take it! The world doesn't move out of the way for wimps. But for the mom who knows who she is and what is rightfully hers, the entire world is in her grasp.

"… Violent men seize it by force [as a precious prize—a share in the heavenly kingdom is sought with most ardent zeal and intense exertion]" (Matthew 11:12 AMPC).

If violent men seize the kingdom by force, violent moms take it a step further. We're violent because we're fighting for more than just us. We're fighting for our families, our inheritance, our tribe. We're fighting for the generations that will come after us, for the ones who will point back to that picture tucked away in the family album and say, "There she is! That was the woman who altered the entire family tree. She broke the curse. She secured the blessing. We are who we are today because she wasn't satisfied with who she was back then. She changed everything."

Get violent, Mama! Roll up your sleeves and take your share of the heavenly kingdom by force. You have every legal right to what is rightfully yours according to the Word and the Will of God. Now receive it! Give yourself permission to live that abundant life that Jesus died for you to have. You've given yourself permission to fail. Now give yourself permission to succeed, and succeed wildly. No, it won't be easy. But you didn't pick up this book for easy. You picked it up for a solution.

God already gave you the solution; I pointed the way. Now it's time to walk it out.

Seize it! It's within your grasp. No, it won't be easy. It takes "ardent zeal" and "intense exertion." In other words, you work your face off. There will be times when it feels impossible, but that's why we don't go by what we feel. We go by what we believe.

I believe in you.
God believes in you.
It's time for you to believe in you.

Keep going. Keep going. And when you don't think you can go any further, take a deep breath, shake it off, and go one more round. Believe you already have everything you seek. Believe you are already the heir of kingdom riches. Believe that the supernatural energy of God Almighty is flooding your body and being. You've been waiting for this moment for years. Lock arms with me, Mama. We're going to do this together.

Mom Fatigue Syndrome.

The real reason you were so tired is that you were trying to carry the weight of the world. But Darling, you were not meant to carry the world, you were designed by God to rule it.